CHANAKYA
IN
LIFE

Radhakrishnan Pillai is the best-selling author of Corporate Chanakya, among many. He is revered across the country not only as an author but also as a motivational speaker. This book is highly anticipated by all his followers as it is the first one that covers topics outside of one's professional life and has a holistic approach towards helping the readers tackle problems that they face on every front.

CHANAKYA
IN DAILY
LIFE

RADHAKRISHNAN PILLAI

RUPA

Published by
Rupa Publications India Pvt. Ltd 2017
7/16, Ansari Road, Daryaganj
New Delhi 110002

Sales centres:
Allahabad Bengaluru Chennai
Hyderabad Jaipur Kathmandu
Kolkata Mumbai

ISBN: 978-81-291-4444-7

Ninth impression 2019

15 14 13 12 11 10 9

Printed at HT Media Ltd, Gr. Noida

*This book is dedicated to those
who struggle to strike a balance in their lives.
And the great Acharya Chanakya, who makes it possible.*

Contents

Introduction

'Who was Chanakya?'

'He was one of the greatest thinkers India has produced. He was a master of many subjects. No, no…I correct myself… he was a master of *all* subjects.'

These were the words of the vice chancellor of a university when he was launching my book.

I had just then completed taking a series of lectures for about 300 students, on Chanakya and his ideas being applied in professional careers.

When the vice chancellor said those words, it hit me hard that there are few parallels in world history who could speak on so many subjects—philosophy, public administration, military, warfare, economics, politics, strategy, taxation, law, crime and control, punishments, duties of individuals, gemology, Ayurveda, Yoga, etc. The list goes on.

Even though in *Arthashastra*, Chanakya has written on 180 topics, there are many sub-topics within each topic. I have personally counted over 1000 topics that Chanakya had spoken and written about. But then, every time I think of any problem I always find a 'Chanakya solution' to it.

When I met Kapish Mehra of Rupa Publications for the first time and discussed the idea of this book, we brain-stormed on many themes.

Finally we decided the theme for this book—Chanakya in daily life.

For me it became easy to focus from that point on. Because when we look into the literature Chanakya had written, it is so vast (6000 sutras in *Arthashastra* and *Chanakya Niti*). So, that just narrowed it down well for me.

'Who would be the readers of our book—the target audience?' was my next question.

'Anyone and everyone who wants to practise Chanakya in daily life—in simple, easy-to-practise steps,' was our conclusion.

Therefore, the book that you have in your hand is simple and profound. Now, anyone can benefit from the wisdom of the great master Chanakya

Chanakya in Daily Life is divided into 3 parts:

- Part 1—Chanakya in Personal life
- Part 2—Chanakya in Professional life
- Part 3– Chanakya in Family life

All of us play these roles simultaneously every day—we have a personal life (only known to us), professional life (involving our work) and family life (the part of our life where we get maximum happiness or sadness from, while dealing with our family members).

Chanakya has spoken on all these topics in detail,

imparting knowledge that will put you on the path to a healthy and happy life.

Balancing these three roles is a challenge to any individual.

At a personal level, one wants to exercise his freedom of choice. But not weighing the impact of his choices on his professional and family life can put him in trouble. He may be labelled a rebel. Individually, the person may be path-breaker, but he might end-up being disharmonious while working with teams.

At a professional level, one may be super successful, have lots of money, power and position. But he may be frustrated and bogged down by the feeling that he could have done better. Probably, there is a sense of incompleteness. Alternatively, he may think that by keeping his family financially well-off, he has done his duty towards them. And later on, he may realize that his wife and kids wanted was to spend more time with him only. But by then, it would probably be too late.

At a family level, one may be an excellent parent and family member. Yet, one might have thoughts like 'What did I do for myself?' There is a sense of frustration one might feel when he sees his siblings better off than himself. This person may have sacrificed his whole life for others, but instead of feeling fulfilled, he feels broken.

This book addresses all these three aspects of life, simultaneously.

And it is possible that one can be successful in all these three roles.

How?

This book gives you the practical route for the same.

Whether you are a student or a married person with responsibilities or a retired person, Chanakya has a message for you.

The most defining part of this book is that, along with giving you tips to improve your daily life, it slowly takes you towards the higher goal of life—spirituality.

While planning your life remember what a wise person said, 'You are not a human being on a spiritual journey. You are a spiritual being on a human journey.'

All great Indian rishis (seers) had a life plan they could chalk out.

Chanakya's 'grand plan' for us is to be successful in this world and also the other world as well.

Arthashastra says,

This science (of *Arthashastra*) brings into being and preserves spiritual good, material well-being and pleasures, and destroys spiritual evil, material loss and hatred (15.1.72)

If you follow Chanakya, when you look back, you will have no regrets. When you are in the midst of your life, you have gathered the required experience, but also have a sense of purpose. If you are still starting off your life, you have planned your life well and you have set a goal, made your roadmap and set towards your life with clarity.

If you have understood this book and its teachings well, you will be like Chanakya, who said, 'Come any problem, in life—I am ready. Because, I know that no problem is a problem for a person who thinks with clarity and purpose.'

Note

Follow these simple steps to get maximum benefit from this book:

- The best part is you can read the book from any chapter. Read one chapter or a few chapters in a day.
- Think and reflect over the ideas you have understood.
- Maintain a dairy and make notes of your progress on a daily basis.
- Discuss these ideas with your family or friends at workplace daily.
- If you are on social media–share your notes and thoughts on Chanakya with others on Facebook, twitter, WhatsApp etc. and spread the message
- Read the book a second time or a third time. Re-reading is encouraged.
- There are many ideas that are repeated in the book at different places. It is not by mistake. It is to make sure you understand the same idea in different contexts. Repetition makes knowledge perfect.

PERSONAL LIFE

1

Waking Up

HAS IT EVER occurred to you that the first thought of your day is the most important one?

'Good morning!' is the way we greet our family members when we wake up.

Be it at school, college or a workplace, we greet each other with this positive phrase.

But what can one do to really *make* the morning good?

In the Indian tradition, we have a method to divinize our thoughts.

We start the day with a sense of gratitude.

Many traditions have specific prayers that should be chanted as soon as one wakes up, while others encourage sitting quietly and meditating for some time before one goes about their daily routine.

Chanakya, who wrote the *Arthashastra*, had some good tips on how to begin one's day. He suggested,

'He (the king) should awaken to the sound of musical instruments.' (1.19.21)

The first book of the *Arthashastra* focuses on the training that the king underwent. It is called 'Vidyasamuddesh'. In it, he shares his knowledge on how to be a good leader. Chanakya also gives practical tips on how to execute one's leadership skills. Note that these tips can also be followed by those who are not leaders, but commoners like you or me. Its beauty lies in the fact that once we follow the tips, we automatically start developing the leadership qualities in us.

The first step of honing one's leadership skills lies in the way we begin our day.

As stated above, Chanakya suggests that one should awaken to the sound of musical instruments. This means that when a person wakes up listening to music, it sets the right mood.

Imagine waking up from a bad dream—the whole day starts on a negative note. You feel drained with every passing minute.

But all that can be corrected just with the sound of musical instruments.

How do we practise this message by Chanakya in our daily life? Here are some tips:

Sleep well

It is not just how you wake up, but also the quality of your sleep that matters. A good seven to eight hours of sleep is essential for an average person. If one sleeps early, and has had an undisturbed sleep, then waking up will be an easy task. It helps one feel energetic and rejuvenated to start the day. So make sure you sleep on time to wake up on time.

Alarm clock

There are two types of alarm clocks one can use for waking up—the external alarm clock and the internal alarm clock. Most of us are aware of the external alarm clock, which rings at a preset time. But do we know about our internal alarm clock?

People who have control over their minds use this alarm clock as well to wake up. They are so disciplined that they instruct their mind, 'Tomorrow morning, I want to wake up at 5 a.m.' and you would be surprised to know that they wake up exactly at 5 a.m. without needing an external alarm clock.

This requires a little bit of practice because you have to keep instructing your mind until it listens. Try it for some time and you will eventually start waking up at the decided time.

Music

For those who use an external alarm clock, the alarm sound is crucial. Nowadays, most of us use the alarm clock on our mobile phones. Choose your alarm tone very carefully. There are various ringtones to choose from. Choose something melodious, for example, an alarm tone that is inspired by nature, like the call of birds or the sound of the wind.

A loud and heavy ringtone will ensure that you wake up, but in a disturbed state. And if there are others in the room, they too will get disturbed. So in general, a loud ringtone will spoil everyone's day.

As Chanakya said, do wake up with the sound of music—but the right music.

Some even start their day with devotional music and spiritual hymns and mantras.

Carry the mood

It is not enough to just wake up in the right mood; one should also carry on in that cheerful mood all day long. Be the source of inspiration to others around you. When you feel good about yourself, you should make others feel good about themselves too. Greet others around you positively.

As the old saying goes, 'The best make-up on your face is a smile.' This will help make sure that your 'good morning' becomes a 'good day'.

2

Music for the Day

LIFE WOULD BE incomplete without music.

Every aspect of our life is connected to music. It might sound strange but the psyche of a person can change, based on the music s/he listens to.

Not everybody can be a singer or play a musical instrument; however, every person can be a listener of music and appreciate its beauty.

Chanakya had used music to develop the personality of a leader. Let us look at what aspects Chanakya focused on.

'Being devoted to the training of the troops, he should arrange signals for the arrays by means of musical instruments, banners and flags, when halting, marching or attacking.' (2.33.11)

Our great acharya suggests that we should play musical instruments even as we go to war.

Any good leader uses musical instruments to train his

troops and discipline them. Even today, the army always has a band of music players. These players compose tunes that uplift the mood of the soldiers. The drums and horns—all help generate enthusiasm in the army, which gets charged up and ready to attack the enemy.

Similarly, even at an individual level, the right use of music can help us improve the quality of our life.

How do we practise music in our daily life in an effective manner?

Time of the day

One has to think carefully before listening to any type of music. Don't just put on the radio or television randomly. Remember, we need to choose our music carefully, as it will invariably influence our personality.

Hold on. Think for a minute.

Decide what kind of mindset you want to create through the music.

The time of the day is an equally important factor. Mornings are very 'sattvic' or pure. This is the time when the mind is most sensitive to the slightest vibrations around. It's best to avoid listening to loud or rock music at this time.

As the day progresses, everyone gets fully charged up. Hence, during the afternoon listen to the kind of music that has a faster pace to match your inner build-up of energy.

Later in the afternoon, after half the day's work is done, one should contemplate on what one's mind needs. If you want to take a nap, listen to soft music. If you want to be active, increase the pace of the music accordingly.

Moods required

One can also create the mood required. For example, if you go to a pub, the mood created there is through a particular kind of music. One is not expected to meditate there, so the music is bound to be loud and encourage dancing.

The background music of movies has a great impact on the viewers. A good music director will always put together the soundtrack carefully.

So use music to create the mood you desire. When you want to have a romantic dinner, choose the appropriate music in the background. If you want your factory workers to be alert at noon, choose music that is of a higher tempo and sounds 'active'.

Now the next step is how to develop an 'ear for music'.

Chanakya had the best of music experts guiding him on this and had access to grand performances in the kingdom.

How do we practise the same in our generation?

Practice of music

Have a good collection of albums, be it on CDs or mp3 files, on your computer or mobile phone. The more the variety of genres, the better it is.

Also, attend music concerts. Keep yourself informed of the artists performing in your city through the newspaper and the Internet.

Learn a musical instrument or even vocal singing. Participate in some musical performance.

On appreciating artists, Kahlil Gibran said, 'And if there

come the singers and the dancers and the flute players, buy of their gifts also. For they too are gatherers of fruit and frankincense, and that which they bring, though fashioned of dreams, is raiment and food for your soul.'

This is why it's important that one pays the musicians and artists well. They are a quintessential part of human development.

And remember, silence is the greatest music.

Sit quietly every day for twenty minutes and listen to your soul.

3

Time for Thinking

THE ABILITY TO think is God's greatest gift to humans.

Other species, too, can think and analyse. However, human beings are far superior in their analytical, logical and creative thinking skills.

Intelligence is, therefore, our most extraordinary asset.

But we seldom exercise our ability to think. We worry instead. Most of us don't know the difference between thinking and worrying.

Worrying is like a rocking chair, it moves but does not go ahead. There is action but no progress.

Thinking, on the other hand, enables one to move forward. From solving problems to creating art, the power of imagination really has no bounds.

According to the *Arthashastra*, we can only achieve our goals through 'anvikshiki'. In other words, clear thinking.

Chanakya suggests that one should have clear thinking from the moment one wakes up in the morning.

He says,

'He should awaken and ponder over the teaching of the science of politics as well as over the work to be done.'
(1.19.21)

No sooner are we awake than our mind is filled with chatter. And this chatter continues for the rest of the day. It is simply the nature of the mind.

But the good news is that we have the freedom to control our minds and steer its thoughts in a positive direction.

Upon waking up, say your prayers and express gratitude. Soon your mind will start to wander...

Stop!

Rather than letting your mind decide where it wants to take you, you lead the way.

Chanakya has suggested two simple steps for this purpose—ponder over the teachings of the science of politics and ponder over the work to be done that day.

Let us see how we can practise this in our daily lives.

Ponder over the science of politics

Arthashastra means 'science of politics', which involves the study of political strategies, systems of governance and the theory of politics; and Chanakya suggests one should ponder over the teachings of the *Arthashastra*. By doing so, one will have a direction on what needs to be accomplished during the day. You will learn how to align and prioritize your activities of the day, take key decisions, etc. based on the tips and guidance given in the *Arthashastra*.

Following this step involves thinking over. One needs to imagine, contemplate and discuss matters with oneself.

Every person is playing a role in life. Often, we have to play multiple roles. As an individual you could be an artist, sportsperson or nature lover. Professionally, you could be a business person, a manager in a company or a self-employed doctor, lawyer or architect. In your family, you could have multiple roles as a parent, a spouse or a homemaker.

As soon as we wake up, all these roles, along with their responsibilities, comes rushing into our minds.

A nature lover would want to watch the sunrise. A health freak would want to go for a morning walk or hit the gym. A business professional would have clients to meet, projects to finish and emails to reply to. A student would have assignments to complete. As a family member, one could have the birthday of their child to celebrate, grocery shopping to do, grandparent's health check-up due, or a family vacation to plan.

Imagine this—every day we're struck by these challenges. And the nature of the challenge keeps changing. So what do we do when all these thoughts start disturbing us every morning?

Ponder over the work to be done

After pondering over all that comes to mind, pause for a moment.

Try to think through this clearly. Not *every* task needs to be worked on immediately. Some can be acted upon later also. Grocery shopping need not be done today itself if there is enough stock for the next two days. College assignments may be submitted after a week.

Therefore, it's crucial that you prioritize what needs to be done right away and what can wait. First thing is to assimilate your thoughts so that you don't miss out on anything. Make a list of the tasks that need to be accomplished. Then prioritize what needs to be done, based on its urgency.

You can make this daily to-do list on a notepad, a computer or even on your mobile phone. Once the priority for the day is set, you will have achieved a degree of clarity that will make you feel you are in charge of yourself and your day.

End the day with a review

Making a to-do list at the start of the day is not enough. One also needs to review it as the day progresses. There is always a possibility of new priorities cropping up, and one may forget to reprioritize accordingly.

Check your to-do list at least three to four times a day and put a tick against whatever is done.

By the end of the day when you review your list, you'll feel confident for having accomplished your tasks in a constructive manner.

Careful planning followed by execution is the key to success.

Swami Chinmayananda used to say, 'Plan out your work, and work out your plan.'

4

Health

YOU SURELY MUST have heard the phrase 'Health is wealth'.

Health is the greatest asset any person can have. If one is healthy, one can do anything. But if one does not have a healthy body and mind, no amount of riches will bring one happiness.

Can one have a healthy body and mind at all times?

Yes, that is possible. Because health is a matter of choice. One can *choose* to be healthy.

But wait. Don't just start doing physical exercise or run a marathon right away. Becoming healthy requires a lot of preparation and planning.

It's all about training.

On this matter, Chanakya said,

'Training and discipline are acquired by accepting the authoritativeness of the teachers in the respective fields.'

(1.5.6)

In the above sutra (formula), Chanakya reveals to us the secret of success in any field of life. He says, to succeed in any field one requires training and discipline.

How does one excel in training and discipline?

By accepting the authoritativeness of one's teachers.

It is a sure-shot formula for success given by Chanakya.

Let us find out how we can plan to be perfectly healthy using the above method:

Set a health goal

One needs to first define what being healthy means to them. Is it losing weight? Or is it getting over some chronic disease which has been affecting you for years? Or is it increasing your stamina and endurance? Or is it getting rid of the long-standing backache?

Once we have defined it, we will have a set goal in mind. But we need to plan how to achieve this goal. And planning is the trickiest part.

How does one come up with a plan to become healthy?

Find a teacher

Yes, this is your next step. Here, a teacher does not mean someone from a school, college or university. You'll need to seek out someone who is an expert in that particular field of health and fitness.

It could be a gym instructor, a yoga teacher, a doctor or a nutritionist. These teachers or gurus have spent years mastering their subject.

For you, becoming healthy is your personal goal. For them,

it is their full-time job to make people healthy. So they have ample experience.

Should we have only one teacher? Not really. It's better if you have a yoga teacher along with a doctor. The yoga teacher will teach you asanas, while the doctor will keep a check on your body readings like blood pressure, sugar level, etc.

Accept authority

It is important to accept your teacher's authority completely. You can't just take some tips from them and not follow it through. You need to accept the fact that your teachers know their job well. Follow their instructions without a doubt and let them work on you.

Today, everything a teacher says is available on the Internet. One just has to google to cross-check what the teachers have told. It is nice to be informed, and a second opinion is always a good idea. But remember, technology cannot replace your teacher. No online courses on health will have the effect that a personal trainer can have.

Even if you are fully healthy, do not neglect your health. Make health your top priority in life.

A wise master once said, 'A healthy person thinks better.'

5

Daily Rituals

ALL OF US practise a set of daily rituals.

How does one define a ritual? It is generally understood as a religious or solemn ceremony. It consists of a series of actions performed according to a prescribed order.

But not all rituals are religious. We wake up in the morning, go to the bathroom and brush our teeth, have a bath, have breakfast and go to work. Most of these rituals are done subconsciously. We hardly put any thought or effort into our daily routine.

Interestingly, management is now considered a science in the field of academics. Experts, scholars and teachers who do research work in this field are called 'management scientists'. Recently, management scientists have proved that rituals are good for us, as they help us lead a disciplined life.

Did you know that Chanakya helped set up a daily ritual for the king? He provided a daily to-do list to his students. Regardless of whether they were kings or leaders, they were supposed to follow those daily rituals.

Rituals are important even to develop leadership qualities in a person.

Therefore the suggestion of Chanakya in the *Arthashastra*:

'And, after going around a cow with her calf and a bull, he should proceed to the assembly hall.' (1.19.24)

The Indian culture has always shown respect towards animals and nature. Many of us even in the modern times follow the religious ritual of praying to the cow.

There is a deeper significance to this ritual.

If a person has an underlying respect for nature, he begins each day with a feeling of gratitude and is at one with God's creation.

This is especially important for people who live in cities. They may be totally cut off from nature but such rituals help them connect to it on a daily basis.

Note here that Chanakya is telling the king to visit the cow, calf and bull before going to the assembly hall. The assembly hall is where official and administrative activities of the king took place. Therefore, Chanakya is suggesting that even before one's official work begins for the day, one should connect to nature.

'Do the most important thing first thing in the morning,' said Swami Tejomayanandaji (from Chinmaya Mission) to his student. 'Later in the day, you will get sucked into the demands of others, and you will never be able to do it.'

That is why Chanakya, too, suggested that all daily rituals be performed in the morning itself.

So how should one practise daily rituals?

Have a ritual

Make a list of the rituals you follow regularly. It could be reading a book, going for a walk, etc. These could even be religious rituals—doing pooja or namaz, reading some verses from holy scriptures, etc.

If you are already doing it—excellent!

If not, make that list and start following it.

In the beginning, practising these rituals will require effort. Make that little effort. Once you get over that stage, you will start enjoying it.

Remember how our parents forced us to brush our teeth when we were kids? Now, we just can't do without it.

Similarly, even religious rituals seem boring in the beginning. But once you've set things in motion, the underlying logic will surface.

Let it become a habit

Once the ritual becomes a habit, then there's hardly any effort required on your part. As mentioned before, at this stage you start enjoying your routine.

Habit can change the destiny of a person and a good habit can go a long way in bettering the quality of one's life.

As an author, I too have a daily ritual of writing for two hours a day. In the initial stages, I did not know how to write for two hours. My mind used to give me reasons not to write, I couldn't come up with new ideas. But then I forced myself to sit for two hours every day just to write and now I do so effortlessly! I enjoy it. In fact, I feel frustrated on the days I do not write.

And look at what a daily ritual turned into a habit has made me—one of India's most successful bestselling authors.

It's self-discipline

A ritual is all about self-discipline. It forces you to do something important on a regular basis. Such daily rituals are healthy for us.

It also has a positive psychological impact. You start mastering your mind, a great task indeed.

A student was once asked, 'How come you top in all your exams?' She gave a great insight, 'I study before exams and during exams. But I study after exams also. In reality, I have started enjoying my studies. It does not matter if studying is for exams or not. I study for the sake of study. It is so much fun.'

So the key is to start enjoying your daily rituals!

6

Astrology

I AM ABOUT to deal with a sensitive topic in this chapter—astrology!

Astrology is connected with astronomy—both are sciences dealing with planets, space and the physical universe as a whole.

Our ancestors were thinkers of the highest level. They knew that the whole world is interconnected. Right from the largest planet to the smallest atom. Nothing and no one exists in isolation. We all are interdependent on each other.

Based on these principles, our rishis developed the science of astrology to guide us through life.

Astrology is called 'jyotish shastra' in Sanskrit. Jyoti (light) and ish (iswara—God). So it means to light up the path that leads to God.

But unfortunately, we look at astrology only in terms of future prediction. It's true that that is a part of astrology, but it is not the ultimate aim of jyotish shastra.

A good astrologer can help you transform your life. They

can lead you from darkness to light.

Therefore, Chanakya suggests meeting an astrologer on a daily basis. He says,

'He should receive (guidance) by seeing his astrologer.'
(1.19.23)

Chanakya himself was an expert astrologer, so he was well-aware of its benefits. That is why he recommended that the king take tips from a good astrologer.

But choosing the right astrologer is crucial. Therefore, an entire chapter in the *Arthashastra* has been dedicated on how to select a raj purohit who has knowledge of the scriptures as also astrology (Book 1, chapter 9—Mantri Purohita Utpatti).

Astrology is never wrong; astrologers could be.

Since astrology is based on calculations, a good astrologer is also a good mathematician. It is a science of permutation and combination.

So how should one go about using astrology to improve the quality of one's life?

Study astrology

Yes. There are books available on the basics of astrology for beginners. Instead of going to an astrologer right away, first read a little bit about it; get familiar with its concept. I am not suggesting you become an astrologer by profession. But it helps if one understands the basic principles of astrology.

Chanakya shared the same belief and hence, included the subject of astrology for kings studying at the gurukul (*Arthashastra* 1.3.3).

Try small tips

Most newspapers carry daily tips for its readers from various astrologers. Paying attention to these columns is a great way of testing the science of astrology and might even help you avert problems. For example, if the weather forecast says it is going to rain, it's better to take the umbrella with you. If it does rain, you not only realize that the weather forecast can be trusted but you also avoided getting wet!

Note that astrology requires a good guide. Otherwise it turns into a mental trap. It is like walking on a razor's edge. You have to be alert about what astrologers are telling you and know how to handle it intelligently. If you are not sure, try out some small tips. Do not follow astrology blindly—you may drown.

Once you start noticing its benefits, you will gain confidence in the field.

Don't depend on astrology

Now this is my final suggestion and it's totally contradicting what was said in the beginning.

Yes, you should explore the realm of astrology but do not fully depend on it!

Chanakya says,

> 'Wealth will slip away from the foolish person who continuously consults the stars; for wealth is the star of wealth; what will the stars do? Capable men will certainly secure wealth at least after a hundred trails.' (9.4.26)

For Chanakya, human effort defines one's destiny. But if a person's destiny is determined by his hard work and commitment, then what can the stars do?

He says, he who 'continuously' consults the stars is a fool.

So after having consulted an astrologer, we should have the inner wisdom to guide ourselves. Respect the tips and guidance given by the astrologer. But remember, your life is in your hands.

Swami Vivekananda put it well: 'There is no greater force in this world than human will, coupled with faith.'

The trick is in knowing how much to take from astrology and how much to let go.

7

Afternoon

MORNINGS ARE USUALLY the time when you do your best work.

It is a time when there are fewer disturbances. Your mood is fresh as you are well rested and you find yourself at the peak of generating great ideas.

But as the day progresses, you get tangled up in the demands of others. Slowly, you lose control of your day.

And then comes the afternoon.

By this time, most of your energy has already been spent on your daily routine.

You are semi-exhausted, if not fully drained of your energy.

A good lunch and probably some discussion with others helps you rejuvenate.

The next two hours are critical. This is typically the lazy period of your day—the afternoon.

What is to be done during afternoons then?

Chanakya advises,

> 'During the remaining part of the day (afternoon), he
> should learn new things.' (1.5.15)

According to Chanakya, afternoons are the best time to learn something new. Why does he say so? Because while the mind can be quite lazy in this period, if you give it a new direction to work in, surprisingly it will cooperate.

In the gurukul, the university of Chanakya, it was suggested that students should study new subjects during the afternoon time. He also suggested that junior students should discuss their doubts with their seniors at this time.

How can we benefit from Chanakya's advice in our daily lives?

Have a hobby

Our lives are dull when we do not engage in anything creative on a daily basis.

Afternoons are the ideal time to pursue one's hobby. It could be an art form like dancing, painting, singing or playing an instrument.

I have known people who take a short break after lunch, even during work days, and go swimming for half an hour. The person returns to his desk productive and efficient.

Read a book

Always carry a book along with you wherever you go.

Read a few chapters of the book every afternoon. Make some notes and, if possible, discuss these ideas with others.

If you develop this habit, by the end of one year, you would have read at least ten to twelve books, which you probably didn't think you had the time for.

You can also watch some educational videos during the afternoon. TED talks are the best. In a matter of twenty minutes, you'd have listened to a world-class expert on their subject. And it'll help you stay up to date on the latest developments across the globe.

Plan a project

Start planning your projects in writing. It could be a vacation, buying a new car, travelling overseas for an educational course—just write down your plan on a piece of paper. These are activities that require time and some effort.

So spend some time on this in the afternoon, and you will be able to foresee challenges and be prepared with solutions.

Meet someone

Any time of the day is a great time to meet friends. But I'd especially recommend afternoons. Be it in your office, home or college—human interaction is always a good thing.

I know someone who built his career just by meeting people in the afternoons.

He said, 'My company was a multinational with lots of employees. It was practically impossible to know everyone. I made a list of the most important people, the ones who would help get my work done. Every day I used to call up a person and go to meet him in the afternoon. I started learning a lot about other fields like finance, marketing, branding, etc.'

He concluded, 'It was like a live classroom every day. I

learnt from many teachers.'

That is basically what Chanakya said—that to succeed in life, one should use one's afternoons productively and engage in new activities.

8

Power Nap

SLEEP—WHAT A BLISSFUL state to be in.

Sleep plays a vital role in maintaining one's health.

The right kind of sleep refreshes and rejuvenates us.

Sleep is now considered a science. Doctors, psychologists and psychiatrists use sleep as therapy for many mental diseases.

In the age of technology, stress is the biggest challenge to most people.

Somewhere in the midst of mankind's progress, our biological clock is getting disturbed. And since we are not in tune with nature's clock, we are facing health problems never seen before.

If you observe any other living creature, you'll find that they all have a natural pattern that they follow to maintain a healthy lifestyle.

Are there tips to live a healthy, natural lifestyle in the *Arthashastra*?

Yes, and it's simple. Chanakya suggests that one should

get the right amount of quality sleep.

He says,

'During the third (part of the night), he should go to bed to the strains of musical instruments and sleep during the fourth and fifth parts.' (1.19.20)

Chanakya had divided the day and night in parts of one-and-a-half hours each.

So he suggests that during the third part of the night, which is, say, from 9 p.m. to 10.30 p.m. one must go to bed. But most of us, when we hit the bed, do not fall asleep immediately. So what should we do to ease the process of falling asleep? Listen to musical instruments before going to bed.

Music has a soothing effect on our mind. The sleep is, thus, peaceful. Remember, there's a good reason why lullabies are sung to children to put them to sleep.

And for how long should one sleep?

Chanakya says, for the remaining two parts. So one has to sleep for three parts of one-and-a-half hours each. From 9.30 p.m. to 1.30 a.m. Total of four-and-a-half hours.

Surprised?

In reality it is not the length of sleep, but the quality of sleep that matters. So if we sleep well this should be enough.

What if our sleep during the night is not enough?

The next suggestion by Chanakya is,

'During the sixth part of the day, he should engage in recreation at his pleasure or hold consultations.' (1.19.14)

Take a power nap in the afternoon.

Chanakya advises that the best time to take a nap is between 1.30 p.m. and 3 p.m. A quick rest in the afternoon goes a long way. And so with another one-and-a-half hours' sleep during the afternoon, a total of six hours of sleep is taken care of.

This amount of sleep is good enough for any average person to feel energetic again.

What if we do not get to sleep in the afternoon?

Here are some practical tips to deal with that:

Go for recreation

Take a break and go for a walk; chat with a friend or even do some yoga asanas; or just sit quietly and meditate; read a book; listen to music. Dedicate this break-time to yourself.

It will, in turn, make you productive for next four hours.

Hold consultation

In case you are fresh and mentally alert, do not force yourself to sleep.

There are always issues where we require guidance from consultants and mentors. Seek an appointment with them. And over a cup of tea, discuss the matters of your concern. As you get new ideas from them, you return to work focused and ready for action.

Make it a daily discipline

Now the key to quality sleep is to sleep on time every night. Chanakya had advised going to bed at 9 p.m. Make the decision to sleep at a fixed time on a daily basis. Discipline is key.

Therefore, the wise saying holds true even today:

'Early to bed and early to rise, makes a person healthy, wealthy and wise.'

9

Study Daily

When we read the word 'study', we usually assume it refers to students only.

But Chanakya tells us that we should be students for life.

Learning is the most important thing in every aspect of our lives. Only through learning do we grow internally and externally.

'The inner world and outer world is the same,' said Swami Vivekananda. So if you have to change your outer world, it is important to first work on your inner world.

The inside manifests itself on the outside.

So change the way you think. Move towards the world of knowledge. Question and reassess your beliefs.

The best way to study is to remind onself that studying is not just for a degree alone.

Unfortunately, our education system has become an examination system.

Yes, one needs to give exams. But don't study only to give

exams. You must develop a passion for knowledge.

Chanakya, therefore, suggested pursuing studies for everyone in any walk of life.

'The duties of a king (leader) are—studying, performing sacrifices for self, making gifts and protecting beings.'
(1.3.6)

Among the various duties prescribed for the king, his first and foremost duty was to study.

Adults may give excuses like they do not have the time or are too busy to study.

But who can be busier than a king or a leader? That person is completely responsible for everything that happens in his or her country or organization.

The king was not given a choice. Studying was his most important duty. Only then could he build a strong kingdom. Today, the world is going towards a knowledge-based economy—a new-age economy based on people who create wealth from knowledge. For example, scientists, teachers, consultants, IT professionals, etc.

Even wealth is created through knowledge. So imagine what a wise and knowledgeable leader can accomplish. S/he will naturally focus on making the world a better place and the citizens more literate and educated.

Chanakya also suggested studying to businessmen, teachers and people in other professions.

'During the third part of the day, he should take his bath and meals and devote himself to study.' (1.19.11)

The instruction continues to suggest studying during the day:

'During the second part of the night, he should take bath and meals and engage in study.' (1.19.19)

In the *Arthashastra*, the Sanskrit word used for 'study' is 'swaadhyaya' (self-study). One has to take interest in studying. The key words here are 'devoted' and 'engaged'.

Once that interest is created, then one naturally feels inspired to pursue knowledge.

So in total, one should study for about three hours every day.

Interestingly, even students these days do not study for three hours a day on a regular basis. Students are supposed to study full-time. But they only study during their exams. After that they forget everything they've learnt.

And here is a leader who possesses the discipline to study every day, irrespective of all the responsibilities on his shoulders.

So let us all make study a part of our daily commitment. Here are some practical tips on how to do that:

Love for books

The first step to study is to develop a love for books. Buy books on topics that interest you and have a dedicated space for them in your home or office.

If not, then at least join a library. It has many benefits—you don't have to spend too much on buying books; you can simply read and return; you don't have to stock books in your house. Most important, with each visit to the library, you stay updated about the latest books, journals and magazines that are being published.

Attend seminars

If you are a student, it is your responsibility to attend all the lectures. But go beyond that. There could be some visiting professors who specialize in certain subjects; try and attend their lectures too.

Even if you have a job, try and attend a seminar or a lecture at least once a month. Many of them take place on Saturdays and Sundays. Better still, become a member of clubs or groups that organize such programmes.

Make notes

Set aside time to study on a daily basis. Start with spending one hour a day. Switch off from technology during this period to avoid distractions from others.

Make notes about what you have studied. This is very important because you can refer to your personal notes in future too. This helps refresh your memory, and you retain what you have studied for a long time.

As management guru Steven Covey said, 'Read deep and read wide. Also, read scholarly and research papers for your personal growth.'

10

Your Swadharma

SWADHARMA IS A SANSKRIT word found in most of the ancient Indian literature.

It consists of two words—swa (oneself) and dharma (something natural).

Therefore, it represents something that is natural to oneself.

Everyone is not created equal. But everyone is unique.

Each one of us possesses something which others do not have—some talent, natural gift or quality.

But unfortunately, instead of focusing on what is good in us, we follow the herd mentality and are always copying others. We compare ourselves against the success of others. Why can't we just focus on what is best suited for us—our swadharma? And also our swabhava (according to our nature)?

Stop following blindly. The real journey in life involves being true to oneself.

Chanakya suggests the same for each of us—to follow a path, a profession that comes naturally to us, something that we can be at ease with.

'The observance of one's own swadharma (special duty) leads to heaven and to endless bliss.' (1.3.14)

When a people finds their natural calling in life, they is bound to find happiness. There could be challenges along the way but nothing would stop them because they're doing the kind of work they love.

For instance, if a person is a naturally gifted painter, they will be happiest when they are painting. Even if in the initial stages there is struggle, it will not affect them much.

One may even get paid lesser in the initial phase but it is only a matter of time before one's talent gets noticed.

All great achievers enjoyed their respective fields of work. They loved what they did and were ready to give up everything for their pursuit.

This is the advice given by Chanakya—to find your calling, your swadharma. Once we have found it, then we are already in the midst of endless bliss.

But the key question remains—how does one find his or her swadharma?

Today, we are living in a world full of opportunities. Having too many opportunities has become a problem rather than a solution, especially for the new generation. For example, students in colleges have many different streams or courses to choose from. People are getting confused and do not know what to do.

Take for instance, a young student who is very good in academics. When that student passes out from school, she does not know which field to pursue in her career. She may get admission into a medical or an engineering college. But maybe she is inclined towards sports.

However, social and peer pressure will not allow her to take up sports as a career. 'You are so good in studies, why go for sports?' would be the first reaction from almost all people.

Then and there would be the demise of a talented sportsperson.

So how do we find a career that will fulfil us?

Observe yourself every day

This method of checking oneself is a good starting point. Observe those moments that bring you happiness in your daily life. It could be anything. For example, if writing makes you happy, probably there is a writer in you who wants to express himself. If you find joy in solving a mathematical equation, you might be a prodigy in math and not even know it.

Follow up your observation with another round of self-check. Are those moments occurring in isolation, just one time, or are they repeating themselves? The resulting pattern will light up the direction you need to move in, in your career.

Check with experts

Being talented is not enough. One needs some form of guidance to become a genius. Go and meet an expert in your field of interest. Discuss and get some inputs. There is no replacement for getting coached and mentored by a guru.

Sachin Tendulkar had a natural flair for cricket. But his talent would not have met with the degree of success it has had his brother not taken him to his coach Ramakanth Acharekar, who made the rough diamond shine on the world stage.

Make it an ambition

Make it your life goal to find your swadharma; go at it with full force. Things don't happen when you wait for them to happen. Take matters in your own hands.

For Steve Jobs, technology and innovation came so naturally that he created a global empire, Apple, out of his passion.

In reality, he had found his swadharma.

Have you found yours?

11

Your Daily Timetable

PLANNING IS THE first step towards success.

When you were a student, your school had a plan for you, one that stretched for many years, from kindergarten to secondary school. Now that you're an adult, do you have a plan for the rest of your life?

Most of us don't.

While it is good to go with the flow, it's also important to be aware of the direction you're moving in. Are you moving in a desirable direction? What is your ultimate goal in life?

If we do not think through these issues, our lives will inevitably be in a mess a few years down the line.

A successful person once said, 'If you fail to plan, you plan to fail.'

Make a list of your priorities and break them down into yearly, monthly and daily goals that will be easily achievable.

In Chapter 19 of the *Arthashastra*, Chanakya guides the king to follow a daily routine, where all his duties are included in a single day.

The day would be full of activities, including meeting citizens, administration, studying, consulting, meeting elders, time for thinking and many other priorities. The idea was that at the end of the day, the king should have achieved all the goals.

But doesn't the daily timetable of a king seem monotonous and rigid? Not at all! It is diverse and flexible.

Chanakya advises:

'Or, he should divide the day and night into different parts in conformity with his capacity and carry out his tasks.' (1.19.25)

Chanakya gives full freedom to adjust this daily routine. He acknowledges that every person's capacity to work differs. Some people are more productive in the morning, while others are in the evening. There are days when one feels like doing more work, while there are days when one feels taking it easy.

So how do we plan our daily timetable as per Chanakya's wisdom?

Make a timetable

It is important to start from where you are. If you feel your life is unplanned, do not worry. Start planning it now. If you do not have a goal in your life, find out what it is now. In case you're wondering—no, it isn't too late. Once you've figured out what you want from life, break it down into daily achievable targets.

For example, before I began writing this book, I broke

up the task into small chapters. Then I prepared the timeline for its completion, which involved me putting in about two hours per day. This made it a lot easier for me to meet my deadline. All my books have been written in record time. It is all due to the advance planning on my part.

Refine it

The daily timetable you prepare should not just cover your work, but make time for all your other roles in your personal and social life. If you focus on just your career, you may succeed in it but might end up losing the respect and love of your family.

And remember, no plan succeeds without perseverance. After you have set a daily timetable, follow it religiously. There might be initial hiccups, but push yourself. You will be rewarded for the same.

See the progress

Once you get a grip on your daily timetable, you will feel confident and in control of your life.

Make note of any progress you make. The more you record your success, the more you will get motivated to continue your pursuit.

Alter it as you grow

As time passes, your daily timetable must change to keep up with your personal growth. It's important that you alter your plans from time to time.

One of the best books on goal-setting is Steven Covey's

The 7 Habits of Highly Effective People. Here, he stresses that goal-setting should be part of your daily routine.

He says, 'Don't prioritize your schedule, but schedule your priorities.'

12

Meditation

Meditation is a very powerful exercise. Many consider it a process that helps one transcend the limits of thought, but it is also a state of mind.

A meditative person is focused, composed, clear and considerate. He knows what to do, and what not to do. He knows when to start, and when to stop.

Meditation is not just something you 'do'. It is also a state of mind to 'be' in, something that you develop throughout your life. You turn meditation into a lifelong experience.

A combination of contemplation (manan) and meditation (dhyana) leads us to a state of mind that is spiritual.

The *Arthashastra* starts with developing the knowledge of anvikshiki. Anvikshiki stands for many things, one of them being philosophical thinking. This can also be interpreted as meditation.

So what are the benefits of regular and deep meditation? Chanakya says,

'Anvikshiki keeps the mind steady in adversity and prosperity and brings about proficiency in thought, speech and action.' (1.2.11)

Here we are not talking about the process of meditation, but its end result. Of course, the highest benefit of meditation is self-realization—moksha, nirvana, jeevanmukti, etc. All these are at the spiritual level.

On the personal front, meditation is the last leap of faith that you take towards yourself—a leap that can benefit you at a worldly level. The first step to achieve success in this world is to have a calm and peaceful mind. Read the above verse by Chanakya again.

He points out that one should meditate to keep the mind steady.

When things are going completely wrong and one does not know what to do, one must find a way to keep calm. But when things are going right and everything seems to be moving in a positive direction, it's still important to keep calm.

And this is achievable through the process of meditation.

When you are relaxed in any situation, it brings about proficiency in thought, speech and action—your thoughts are clear, you speak without confusion and your actions lead to success.

As the Bhagwad Gita says, '*Yoga Karmasu Kaushalam.*' Yoga brings excellence in whatever you do.

As a beginner, here are some basic tips to help you meditate:

Sit quietly

The first step in meditation is to sit quietly in one place. Start with fifteen minutes a day and slowly, over a period of time, make it about half an hour, or even one hour.

Choose a time slot, preferably in the morning, and sit down in a comfortable place and position. Try not to change the place. This will help train your mind to be at the same place and the same time each day.

Keep all gadgets and other unnecessary distractions away from you. Do request your family members not to disturb you during that time.

Relax and observe your mind

Take a few deep breaths. Relax your mind and body. Positive affirmations like 'I am relaxed', 'I am calm', 'I am quiet' all help one feel calm.

Now watch your mind. Start praying to God. Since you are new to meditation, a small prayer asking for help from the Almighty is always a good thing. Surrender.

No mind

Your thoughts will start receding. This is the time to be alert. In this relaxed state, it's imperative that you resist any urge to fall asleep. It is natural for a relaxed and calm mind to want to take a nap. But that is the opposite of meditation, which is a state of complete alertness.

Keep doing this and try to be in the state of no mind and no thoughts for as long as you can.

When you are done, try to keep yourself calm as much as you can even after leaving your seat of meditation.

This state of mind will carry itself forward onto your work and the rest of your activities. And you will improve on every front. You will even have revelations.

Srinivasa Ramanujan, the great Indian mathematician, used to pray and meditate and he could crack the mathematics of the universe. He once said, 'An equation means nothing to me unless it expresses a thought of God.'

Finally, don't give up. There could be some failures in the beginning. But the secret of success is to continue meditating until you succeed.

13

Food

THE ESSENCE OF a person greatly depends on the kind of food he consumes.

There are two types of food—the physical food that we eat, and the food for thought.

The real wisdom lies in choosing your food carefully. Right food consumed in the right manner can help transform the health of your mind and body.

All medical institutions across the globe know that along with medicines, the food that is consumed is equally important in curing any disease.

Chanakya was an expert in the science of food. He had thoroughly researched food and its consumption. He did it not only for human beings, but for animals and plants too.

Throughout the *Arthashastra*, he gives tips on what types of food are to be consumed.

The first advice given to a king is to meet the cook on a daily basis:

'During the eighth part of the day, he should see his chief cook.' (1.19.23)

As part of his routine, the king must go and meet his chief cook each day.

The chief cook was someone who had in-depth knowledge of everything that went into preparing a royal meal—from the raw ingredients to the supply systems, from how to source the best fruits, vegetables and spices to the finances involved. He understood the impact of seasons on his raw material. He could also differentiate between original and duplicate items.

All governments have policies that focus on providing quality food to its people. For example, in India, food security is a basic right for every citizen. Plus, now we are also focusing on providing food that is nutrition-centric, to solve the problem of malnutrition in the country.

Similarly, in the king's case, the chief cook was responsible for the overall health of his kingdom. And, therefore, a daily meeting with the chief cook was essential for the king.

But what can we do at an individual level regarding our diet?

Do some shopping

Now, this is the best thing you can do to learn about the most important part of food—the ingredients. Take a trip to the local market and observe what kind of vegetables, fruits, pulses, grains and spices are being sold.

Listen carefully to the discussions between shopkeepers and buyers. Understand from where the ingredients are sourced. Understanding the food industry will also help you understand the economics of it—the concept of demand and supply.

Try making something

Now that you have understood how things *work*, try to actually *make* something. The best way to understand food is to make it yourself. Become a chef for a day.

There is no better expression of love towards any of your family members than trying out a recipe for them. This is a great experiment not only in terms of cooking but also as an act of love.

Last but most important—wherever and whenever you travel, try to eat what the locals eat. And in a country like India, there is no dirth of variety in food.

The best way to discover a place is through its food.

And the best way to a person's heart is through the stomach!

14

Self-discipline

THERE ARE TWO types of discipline—external discipline and internal/self-discipline.

Discipline may be enforced externally in the beginning, say, by a teacher in school, or a boss at work, or a parent at home. But, in the long run, the external discipline should be internalized and turned into self-discipline.

For example, in your initial phase at work, the rules of the company or organization will force you to be punctual and achieve the targets set for you. Your boss may monitor and even do a micro-review of your work. But once experienced, you will have to take the initiative yourself.

Chanakya had a similar method to discipline a king.

He would keep a minister in charge to discipline the king, especially on time management.

'He (king) should set the preceptors or ministers as the bounds of proper conduct (for himself), who should

restrain him from occasions of harm, or when he is erring
in private, should prick him with the goad in the form
of indication of time for the performance of his regular
duties by means of the shadow of the water clock.' (1.7.8)

This is a beautiful method through which Chanakya is
imposing external discipline on the king. When one is not
sure if one can follow discipline on one's own, it's good to
appoint a trusted person to remind one.

The preceptor (teacher) or any other trusted person was
told to set a proper boundary, and not to cross the limits.
They were empowered to restrain the king whenever there
was a possibility of harm. So even in private if he was doing
something wrong, they were advised to prick him with a goad
(rod).

The king had many meetings with people of higher
positions. There was a natural tendency for one meeting to
exceed and spill over into the next meeting. So a soft reminder
from the teacher or minister helped. They did this by showing
a clock to the king.

But finally, Chanakya says that over a period of time, all
this should translate into self-discipline.

'One doing whatever pleases him does not achieve
anything.' (7.11.35)

Here, Chanakya is stressing on the importance of controlling
one's mind. The mind has a tendency to do as it pleases. A
person who does whatever pleases his mind does not achieve
anything.

This is where self-discipline comes in.

Decide what is to be done, then go ahead and achieve it.

Here are some simple steps we can follow to achieve self-discipline:

Have a clear agenda or goal

One has to have a clear goal in mind, for starters. If the agenda itself is not there, then we end up feeling purposeless. So it's important to set a goal that our mind can focus on.

For example, say, you need to lose ten kilos. Now that you have that aim, draw up a plan on how you will achieve it—a diet plan, an exercise routine, etc.

Share it with someone close

Make sure you have a friend with whom you share your goals. And then ask the person to help you monitor your progress. It could be your gym instructor, your spouse, your brother or even a colleague.

Make sure these are people you trust, because you're essentially asking them to be your partner in achieving your goal. They should be given the freedom to correct you without you feeling offended.

Try on your own

There comes a time when you have to try doing things on your own. Can you get up without the alarm clock? Can you get into office on time without your boss asking you to be punctual? Can you complete your homework without the threat of punishment from the teacher?

Once such a state of self-motivation is achieved, you automatically become an inspiration to others around you.

Then others will seek your guidance on the path to success and self-discipline.

15

Find Your Pattern

PATTERNS EXIST EVERYWHERE.

For example, all successful people have patterns.

Steve Jobs had a pattern in the way he dressed up—he always wore a black turtleneck with jeans.

Sachin Tendulkar had a pattern of batting well against spin bowlers.

Everyone has a pattern. Many people like to go for a walk every day at the same time and on the same route.

Even nature works in patterns—seasons, sunrise, the blooming of flowers—everything happens at the right time. And farmers know this all too well, for it aids their harvest.

Patterns are useful, because they free the mind from using energy for routine work. The way this works is that since the mind has a tried-and-tested pattern that it can blindly follow, it can instead focus on other, more innovative work.

One of the first steps towards success in life is to recognize your pattern.

Someone once said that the most productive years of a person is between the ages of forty to sixty. At forty you are not inexperienced. You have a good sense of what life is all about. But you also have twenty more productive years ahead of you.

So recognizing the pattern of your life at forty sets you on the path towards a higher, purposeful life. A midlife crisis can become a midlife boon.

Chanakya advises the king to follow a pattern in his daily activities. He says,

> **'He should divide the day and night into eight parts, as also the night by means of nalikas (time measurement).'**
> **(1.19.6)**

Here we see the pattern being created by Chanakya for the king.

First, divide the twenty-four hours of your day into day and night. Divide the day into eight parts and the night into another eight parts. So, in total, a day of twenty-four hours is divided into sixteen parts. Each part is of one-and-a-half hours each.

Now decide what you want to accomplish in that day. Then you can fit in every task in the pattern of one-and-a-half-hour units and have a clearer schedule in mind.

This pattern of one-and-a-half hours is very relevant in our age and if you observe, you'll find this pattern everywhere. It has been scientifically proven that an average person can focus on one thing for a maximum of ninety minutes. After that, it becomes rather difficult to continue.

And so, it makes sense why the length of an English film

is usually made of one-and-a-half hours long, in other words, ninety minutes. A Bollywood film usually lasts for about three hours, with an interval after one-and-a-half hours.

Even in higher education in universities, lectures usually last for one-and-a-half hours.

So Chanakya's advice, to put it simply, is to take a break and come back to that work with renewed concentration. How should you set patterns in your lives?

Make a list of your personal goals

This list could be personal or professional. Do prepare a list, if you do not have one already. Then prioritize each task and set a time limit to achieve each goal; and then put them into slots of ninety minutes each.

But it is imperative that you set your goal first.

Do it in chunks of ninety minutes

For example, when I set out to write a book, the first thing I do is set a deadline for its completion. I divide the book into sections and put them into ninety-minute time slots.

So in total I work for three hours every day, with a break after every ninety minutes. When the day is more relaxed, I write for three to four sets of ninety minutes each. I may even write for six hours a day without getting tired.

Include everything

Don't get fixed on one thing and put aside everything else. An ideal pattern is one where you include time for relaxation too.

Set aside ninety minutes every day for exercise or spending

time with your family. Or read every day for those ninety minutes. You will find your productivity at a personal level reaching greater heights with every passing day.

Here's a secret—the universe is full of patterns. To understand it, you first need to understand its patterns.

Our life is simply a reflection of the universe it exists in.

So set a pattern for yourself, and be one with the flow of the universe.

16

Creative Hobby

MANY CONSIDER A hobby as something that is just for passing time.

They're wrong. A hobby makes effective use of time by helping one create something.

If you look at the definition of a hobby, it means an activity or interest pursued for pleasure or relaxation and not as a main occupation. Gardening, reading, singing, are all considered hobbies that people do, other than their professional work.

But the truth is, if you follow your hobby diligently, it might end up being more productive than your main occupation.

All great people have hobbies. J.R.D. Tata, the famous industrialist, liked listening to music from across the globe. Homi Bhabha, the great nuclear scientist, enjoyed painting. Albert Einstein, the world-renowned physicist, played the violin and piano, apart from sailing and writing travelogues.

The various hobbies Chanakya suggested to a king included listening to musical instruments, swimming and hunting.

For hunting, which was a game during those days, Chanakya suggested,

'He should go to a forest containing game, for practising on moving targets.' (1.21.23)

Most countries have now banned hunting as a leisure activity.

But we need to look at Chanakya's suggestion from a different perspective.

The above suggestion for hunting does not suggest the act of killing an animal or bird. It simply says to practise on a moving target.

A king in those days was also expected to be a great warrior. So during leisure time he was supposed to hunt and even catch animals. But it was not an easy task. An animal from the forest understands its habitat better than humans and knows all its routes. If you try to catch it, it can easily escape. There is also the danger of the hunter becoming the hunted. So it is all a mind game and requires a foolproof strategy if one is to win. And this was where the king's training came into play.

Similarly, this logic is applicable to other hobbies as well. If you take up gardening, you should research seasons and their impacts on plants. If you take up an instrument, you should hone your ability to differentiate between notes and scales. Whatever you do, acquire a holistic understanding of your hobby.

So you see, hobby is a serious activity. Except, it is not stressful. It actually de-stresses you.

So what should one keep in mind while developing a hobby?

It is important

Having a hobby in itself is important. It is something we should all develop in our lives. Just as reading and writing helps us in all walks of life, a hobby too helps us develop certain skills required in life.

It is also important to upgrade yourself in your hobby. Suppose your hobby is to play the flute; do not play the same tune every day even after twenty years. This would drain the creativity of this activity. So keep improving your hobby. Listen to new tunes, learn new dance pieces. Whatever your hobby, keep learning.

It refines you

A hobby helps sharpen the mind. But it is only over a period of time that you'll be able to appreciate the finer aspects of your hobby. Your mind will become more alert and receptive.

If reading is a person's hobby, subconsciously the person is bound to start understanding the patterns of various books. He is soon able to differentiate between good and bad books. This type of insight can be developed through a hobby in other fields too.

Give it time regularly

Don't leave a hobby midway. Give it time every day. Some people follow a hobby religiously during their childhood, but they do not continue it into adulthood. There are few things sadder than the death of creativity.

So follow your hobby and give it your best. Who knows,

you might just make a fulfilling career out of it! And if not, then remember that life without a hobby is dull and boring. Whenever you feel down and low, you will always have your hobby to go back to.

17

Personal Finances

THE GROWTH OF a person is measured in various ways—the education one receives, the position one holds in his career, how well respected one is in society, and most importantly, how much money one has.

We cannot call ourselves fully successful till we are able to create wealth and manage our personal finances.

The *Arthashastra* itself can be translated as a book on wealth, finance and economics. Artha (wealth) and shastra (scripture) stands for wealth of knowledge and knowledge of wealth.

The 6,000 sutras given in the *Arthashastra* itself reveal to us many secrets of getting rich. It is one of India's finest contributions to the world. Chanakya says,

'Easy to learn and understand, precise in doctrine, sense and word, free from prolixity of text, thus has this work (Arthashastra) on the science been composed by Kautilya.'

(1.1.19)

When we think of studying the *Arthashastra*, the first thing that comes to our mind is, 'It is going to be very difficult'. This is not true. Chanakya himself has said in the above verse that it is easy to learn and understand and not at all confusing.

But then, how do we explain our mental block? It is because the *Arthashastra* has not been projected in the right manner to us. Also, we do not learn it under the guidance of a proper teacher who has studied and understood it.

So, I'm taking the opportunity to simplify the *Arthashastra* and its financial models in four easy steps for you to practise at the personal level. Here they are:

Wealth identification

The first step is to identify where money will come from. If we observe ourselves carefully, we shall find that each of us has a unique talent or God-given gift through which we can become rich. Unfortunately, most of us aren't able to identify that uniqueness in ourselves.

In today's day and age, it is all about specialization. An expert is paid more than the other people in that field because he is privy to the knowledge that most of them seek. So, try and become a specialist in your area of interest. Instead of going after money, identify your inner wealth and money will automatically follow you.

Develop your inner capabilities, get educated and learn from other experts. One day, without you even being aware of it, opportunities will come knocking at your door.

Wealth creation

Just because we are good at something does not mean we will become rich. One has to work hard to create wealth.

Keep your eyes and ears open for different possibilities. Swami Chinmayananda put it well, 'When opportunity knocks at the door, either we have gone outside, or are sleeping inside'. Be very alert and grab the chance before others do.

If you truly put in your best, others will inevitably think of you as a person with quality output. You will get more and more offers if you are known as a person who delivers results on time.

Wealth management

Once you start making money, do not get excited. It is important to start saving right away. This is where wealth management comes into the picture.

Nowadays, one can take advice from professional wealth managers. There are various schemes where you can save and invest. Mutual funds, insurance plans, shares of companies, investment in real estate—there is no dearth of options.

Remember, the good days may not last forever. So it's important to start saving and investing for the bad days during the good days itself. For instance, many who win the lottery start spending excessively and instead of staying wealthy they land up being poor again.

Wealth management skills will help you stay rich forever.

Wealth distribution

Saving and investing your money does not mean you should not spend at all. Do not become a miser. That is not the point. Personal finance has to be managed well. Then look at how you can give back to society and the not-so-fortunate people.

We are all products of society. Our parents, family members, society, the government, all have spent a lot on us. They educate us, provide us safety and security, and enable us to be citizens of this world. Now, it is time we give back to them.

There is a Personal Social Responsibility (PSR) each one of has—to make sure we do not die as someone who was rich, but someone who made *others* rich.

The wealth we give others comes back to us in some way or the other. And it stays with us permanently.

So use these principles from the *Arthashastra* and watch your personal finances grow exponentially.

18

Life Plan

HUMAN LIFE IS a gift from God.

Out of all the species on earth, we are the privileged ones.

Like other species, we can think, but we can also create, visualize and most importantly, achieve the highest state of consciousness—self-realization.

But should we have a plan in life, or just go with the flow?

We need to balance both—plan our lives and let life flow through us.

Our ancient Indian Vedic culture had a broad vision of life. Right from birth to death, it gave us a systematic way to lead our lives.

Chanakya, too, emphasizes the importance of planning one's life in the *Arthashastra*. He urges one to re-establish the Vedic life pattern by saying,

'The law laid down in the Vedic lore (tradition) is beneficial, as it prescribes the respective duties of the four stages of life.' (1.3.4)

The Indian tradition derived its wisdom from experiments carried out across generations and was intended to benefit mankind at large. This was done so that the following generations would not make the same mistakes. And in the *Arthashatra*, Chanakya has bifurcated life into four phases and given us clear directions to follow in each phase if we are to live a fulfilling life.

What are those four stages of life?

The life plan given in Indian culture is divided into four stages—a student, a householder, a retired person and a monk.

Let us assume that each person lives for a hundred years. The four stages can be divided into an average of twenty-five years each.

Now let us see what is expected to be done in each of these four stages of life:

Student life (Brahmacharya-ashram)

The first stage of life, this is when we get ready to face the world. Recognizing how crucial these formative years are, our ancient education system focused on giving a child both spiritual as well as worldly knowledge.

Our great teachers, including Chanakya, created a beautiful education system, laying the very foundation of what is today the modern society.

So it's important that you get the best education possible. But please remember, the best education does not mean schools with flashy infrastructure and high fees. It is the quality of teachers that's most important, for they are the ones who will enable you to plan out your life.

Householder's life (Grihasta-ashram)

This is the second stage where one gets married and takes up various family responsibilities. Taking care of elders and the children in the family, earning money, managing finances and doing a job—all have to be done simultaneously. So it requires a lot of energy and commitment to be successful at this stage of life.

The key to a successful marriage is a good life partner. If your spouse is also a good friend, then your journey at this stage will be a lot smoother.

But remember, in this stage of life, you must be ready to give more than your 100 per cent. Be a committed partner. Look after your elders. Educate your children and prepare them to stand strong in the face of challenges.

Retired (Vanaprastha-ashram)

By the time you enter this stage of life, your children will have grown up and probably be married, shouldering their own responsibilities. This is the time you are a bit relaxed. Your duty is just to watch them as they make their own choices, and spend some good time with your grandchildren.

Please remember that you should provide guidance only when asked for it. Do not try to interfere in others' lives. It helps to be detached.

In the olden days, many people chose to retreat into a forest and spend their time meditating. Today, we have the choice to go away from our families to spiritual places and lead a life of spirituality.

Monk (sannyasa--ashram)

This stage is also known as sannyasa or parivrajaka-ashram. When one enters this stage, one completely cuts off all worldly ties. There is no contact even with family members. One is supposed to become a wandering ascetic.

In most religions of Indian origin, there is an allusion to this stage in one way or the other. One takes on monkhood under the guidance of a guru. And its sole purpose is to realize God.

We can also use the last stage of our life for our spiritual development. With no regrets or unfulfilled desires, one waits for a glorious exit from this world.

Try to follow Steven Covey's advice. He said, 'Begin with the end in mind.' What this means is one should visualize oneself being taken away on their funeral. At the moment when you visualize that, ask yourself—looking back, if you could choose, what kind of life would you have wanted to live?

Start living that kind of life. Right now.

19

Become an Institution

CHANAKYA'S LIFE IS an inspiration.

He was able to make himself an institution. His journey from being an individual to becoming an institution is worth studying.

While we're all in awe of him, each of us has the capabilities to be a Chanakya in our respective fields.

Upon understanding Chanakya, you will want to contribute to society in a way that the generations to come will remember your work.

Most importantly, he wrote the *Arthashastra*.

> 'This science (Arthashastra) has been composed by him, who in resentment quickly regenerated the science and the weapon and the earth that was under the control of Nanda kings.' (15.1.73)

The last king of the Nanda dynasty, Dhana Nanda was a corrupt ruler. Chanakya defeated and dethroned Dhana Nanda and made Chandragupta Maurya the king. And then he wrote the *Arthashastra*.

Generation after generation, his secrets on good governance have been used by various kings. Millennia have passed and still Chanakya continues to inspire us.

What are the teachings from his life that will help us start our journey from being an individual to an institution?

Do something extraordinary

To think small is a crime. Dr A.P.J. Abdul Kalam told us to dream big and aim for the skies. The same was reflected in the life of Chanakya—an ordinary teacher who did extraordinary work. Chanakya had taken up a challenge that few people would even think of. He challenged the Nanda king of the most powerful dynasty at that time. Chanakya was not a king himself, nor did he have an army. But he took up the task and achieved the goal of defeating him.

Next, he took up the challenge of defeating Alexander, another powerful king on his way to conquer the world. With his ordinary student force, led by a village-dweller Chandragupta, he brought the Greek invaders to their knees.

Let us learn from Chanakya's actions. He shows us that in life one should set a high target and make the impossible possible. You cannot afford to underestimate yourself.

Inculcate a thirst for knowledge

The best way to create a legacy is to inculcate a thirst for knowledge. Teach people what you've learnt in life. Pass on your experience. They will take your work and vision forward.

You will leave the world one day, but your life's work will live on through these students.

Like Chanakya, if you can build an educational institution, a gurukul, it will be a phenomenal achievement.

If you cannot build an educational institution yourself, teach in an existing one. Chanakya taught in Takshashila University before creating a gurukul of his own. Giving back to students what one has learned is a great way of taking knowledge forward.

Create systems and processes

Chanakya believed in the importance of having efficient systems and processes in place. He created instruction manuals for leaders to follow. In the *Arthashastra*, one can learn about the intricacies of how an ideal kingdom is created and governed.

Great thinkers don't come up with ideas, they come up with *realistic* ideas. And then they also help build a system in place to let those ideas flourish.

In your life, you must aim to do the same. And the best part is that you have technology at your disposal to make this happen.

Write a book

This is the best way to tell your story to others.

If you have thoughts like 'Who will read my book?' then please stop that voice in your head right now.

Imagine, what if Chanakya had not written the *Arthashastra*? We would have lost all his knowledge to doubt. In fact, I would not have been able to write this book either, had I entertained such doubts. So remember, there are readers out there waiting to read your story.

My advice for beginners would be to maintain a daily journal. Jot down everything you learn each day. This is best done at night before going to sleep.

Try this for a month and you will see that there is so much you have learned. After a year you will find that your diary and its notes are your real assets. Something no one can take away from you, for knowledge documented is permanent knowledge.

Live to inspire.

20

Personal Guru

THE CONCEPT OF a personal coach is rather common in the field of sports. Any successful sportsperson knows the importance of his/her personal coach. If you hit the gym, a personal coach can help accelerate your progress. He will guide you as per your specific requirement.

In a similar manner, there are coaches, mentors and guides in every other field. In India, such teachers, experts and guides are known as gurus.

There are business coaches, political mentors and technical consultants. In India, we also have spiritual gurus.

What is the role of these people?

To help and guide you at every step.

If Chandragupta Maurya hadn't received personal guidance from Chanakya, he would not have become one of the greatest emperors of India.

So the question is, how do you find your personal guru? Let us start with what Chanakya had said about these gurus,

> 'When he (prince) is ready for it (knowledge), experts
> should train him.' (1.17.27)

A king became a king because he adhered to the guidance of
a guru himself. When a king's own child was groomed to take
over his throne, there were experts appointed to train him in
the science of raja-niti.

Similarly, in today's world, when the child is ready to start
learning, parents try to provide him with the best education,
good school and even private coaching classes if need be.

Also, when the child is interested in other fields like
sports, foreign languages, arts, etc., they are sent to the relevant
institutions.

Whatever may be the case, Chanakya says that it is crucial
that we have a good guide/trainer/guru early on. So here is
what we can do:

Make a list

While there is a particular field we have chosen for our career,
we're all simultaneously involved in various activities that are
related to other fields. This is because apart from our job,
there are things of genuine interest that we like to spend time
doing and don't mind putting effort into. Make a list of all
these interests.

So if you are a software engineer working in a company,
that is your area of work. But apart from that, you may also
be interested in swimming, playing the piano or trekking.

Now, you need to think about being an achiever in every
field you get into. So, if you are starting your career as a
software engineer, good. But don't be content with just that.

Aim to become a project leader in your company who heads various software development projects.

And along with this, when you play the piano, aim to be the best. Or if you are a trekker, aim to climb Mount Everest one day.

Find a guru

Now, after making the list, try to find the gurus for each field. How should you do that? First, think about what would be required of you to excel in each field. What are the skills required for me to become a project leader? How is a good piano piece constructed? What are the basic requirements of a trekker who wishes to climb Mount Everest? Read a bit on all these topics.

Then research on personal gurus in each field.

It may seem difficult in the beginning, but keep on searching. Seek and you will find. When the student is ready, the guru arrives.

Attend a course

Once you have found the right guru, attend the courses they conduct. A good piano player is likely to be a teacher as well. Take some lessons from them. Someone who has climbed Mount Everest would be happy to share his experience with other mountaineers.

A project leader in your office may not conduct a formal course on project leadership. However, you can request for a personal sitting and guidance. It can be during non-office hours.

When I wanted to study the *Arthashastra*, there was no formal course available anywhere. I approached the Chinmaya International Foundation, where Swami Advayananda found a personal teacher for me—Dr Gangadharan Nair, a great Sanskrit scholar, who taught me all the 6,000 sutras in the book. One teacher. One student. The course was customized for me.

Seek and you will find it.

Be in touch

Practise the skills you learn on a daily basis, whatever they may be. Take a few measures to improve your project. Practise the piano often. Get yourself ready to climb Mount Everest.

Whatever be your progress, keep your guru informed. Only if you are in regular touch with your guru will s/he be able to guide you further.

Your guru may also give you some personal contacts to help you reach your goal faster.

And one day you will achieve excellence. What next?

Become someone else's guru. And share the knowledge you gained along the way. It's your turn now.

21

Practical Philosophy

WHEN WE TALK about philosophy from a Western standpoint, it seems very abstract and other-worldly. But our ancient teachers believed that if philosophy is not practical, then it is not real philosophy. Therefore, they designed the Indian philosophy in a manner that it could be used in one's daily life too, which is what makes it a 'practical philosophy'.

Chanakya had spoken of anvikshiki (philosophy) as the foundation of a good king. The concept of a philosopher-king (raja-rishi) was what he had in mind.

However, it's not only a king or a leader who must be philosophical. Even the common man should have some foundation in philosophy.

Another word used for philosophy in sanskrit is dharma, which also translates to natural laws that govern an individual and society.

The four purusharthas (aims of life) include dharma (philosophy), artha (aim/meaning), kama (desires) and moksha (freedom).

In the next few chapters we will see how these four purusharthas can be practised in our personal lives on a daily basis.

So let us begin with dharma in this chapter.

The word 'dharma' comes up over 150 times in the *Arthashastra*, suggesting various ways in which we can apply this philosophy in our lives. On dharma, Chanakya says,

'Anvikshiki (practical philosophy) helps us investigate by reasoning the difference between dharma (spiritual good) and adharma (evil) as per Vedic tradition.' (1.2.11)

One needs to first know what the word dharma exactly means. If not understood properly, it becomes 'dharma-sankat', meaning moral dilemma.

To be or not to be, that is the question—a moral dilemma raised by William Shakespeare in his famous work, *Hamlet*.

But Chanakya is very clear as far as dharma is concerned. He says that you should use anvikshiki (logical thinking) to pursue dharma in life. Use reasoning and investigate the different aspects of a situation properly before taking a decision.

Here's how you can use dharma or philosophy in a practical way:

Do good work

The most important endeavour of your life should be to do good work. How should you go about it as an individual? Well, there are many individuals and organizations that do great social work. You could be part of the countless NGOs that are doing dharmic work and could use more volunteers.

Not only will you be contributing to the greater good of society, but you will also start to feel good about your selfless deeds.

I have a friend who started one such organization that engages in social service. His NGO is called 'Your Turn Now'.

Remember all the times someone did something good for you. Now take that gratitude you're feeling and redirect it outwardly. Go ahead. Do something for someone else today. Spread that seed of compassion and watch it grow and blossom in fellow human beings.

No philosophy in the world is complete if it does not serve the greater good of mankind.

When in conflict

There's a chance that while doing good work you may be confronted by moral conflicts. You may start to wonder what any of it means. If there's any higher purpose at all. You may start to wonder about the meaning of your existence and start questioning the concepts of 'good' and 'bad'.

Chanakya has advised us to 'think' through the conflict first. What is the moral conflict all about? Is it imaginary or real? Are there proofs regarding the same? Who is on the wrong side and who is on the right side? Is it spiritually good? Does it bring benefit to anyone? All this must be investigated by means of reasoning. It is a logical, step-by-step process.

Now, just because it is a moral dilemma, do not stop doing the good work. If you want more clarity on the issue, follow the next step.

Take advice

Dharma sankat can be resolved through discussions with wise people. Your elders and other experienced folks will show you the way. There are people who have walked this path before you. Seek and take their advice.

The famous moral dilemma or dharma sankat comes in the midst of a battlefield in the Mahabharata. Arjuna, the best warrior, developed cold feet just as the war was about to begin. He was not sure about what to do and what not to do.

But running away was not the solution. He had to face it. And this was part of the famous advice given by his friend and charioteer, Lord Krishna, in the form of the Bhagwad Gita.

And, having clarity on what was right and what was wrong, Arjuna got up to fight. With the help of Krishna's strategies, he won the war, which was rightly called 'dharma yudh' (a war of righteousness).

Once, a confused disciple asked his guru, 'What is to be done when you do not know what is right and what is wrong?'

The guru smiled as he said, 'Follow your heart.'

The heart, your inner voice, always knows right from wrong.

Listen to that voice.

22

Fulfil Your Desires

IT IS NATURAL to have desires. But one mustn't get carried away by them.

The Indian culture does encourage fulfilling one's desires but also shows us how to find a balance in doing the same.

Much of our dissatisfactions arise from unfulfilled desires. But neither can you suppress, nor would it possible to fulfil, each and every one of them.

So what is the solution?

You must fulfil your desires in an ethical manner. Once we know the method of doing that, then we do not feel guilty of being in abundance and richness. We're able to detach ourselves from our pleasures. Chanakya suggests that you start small.

He says,

'He should enjoy sensual pleasures without contravening his spiritual good and material well-being; he should not deprive himself of pleasures.' (1.7.3)

Here, the great Chanakya is guiding us on something very important. He says that no one should deprive himself or herself of the pleasures of life. But there is a warning in there too. He should enjoy these pleasures without being at odds with spiritual good and material well-being. This would involve fulfilling these pleasures in a dharmic manner, with hard-earned money.

In the discussion in the *Arthashastra*, there is a debate on 'dharma', 'artha' and 'kama' that helps shed light on how one must fulfil pleasures. The overall conclusion is—kama (desires) should be based on dharma (spiritual good) and artha (material well-being).

Let us see how we can apply this principle in our lives:

Earn with integrity

There is nothing wrong with desiring wealth, luxury and a comfortable lifestyle. But what method you use to fulfil these desires is crucial. It has to be done through the right methods of earning.

So earn with integrity. Be honest about the way you make your wealth. It takes time to create a big amount of wealth through the right methods. But it is worth the effort.

Indian scriptures mention two paths towards success—shreyas (path of good) and preyas (path of pleasure).

Shreyas is the right path, but also a long and hard one. In the initial stages you may feel you are not moving close to your goal at all. But be patient, because once you get there, that success will be permanent.

The path of preyas is one that is full of shortcuts and

requires less effort. In the beginning, it may give one the illusion of success. But since this path is not based on natural principles, failure is bound to happen. As a master once said, 'The longest route to success is a shortcut.'

Spend with compassion

Don't be a miser. Be ready to spend what you have rightfully earned. Chanakya is not suggesting that you become a spendthrift. But not spending at all is also not good.

So spend what's needed to fulfil all your desires. Spend on others as you do on yourself. There is a famous instance of Swami Vivekananda meeting John Rockefeller, one of the richest Americans in Chicago. Swami Vivekananda advised Rockefeller to give back his wealth to the society. He said, 'Wealth should be like breeze—it should come from one window and go out from another.'

Inspired by the thoughts of the saint, Rockefeller went on to become one of the greatest philanthropists of his generation. The Rockefeller Foundation continues to do great work to this day.

Have luxuries

To live in palaces and be surrounded by wealth is excellent. Prosperity is encouraged. Wealth even takes the form of a goddess in India—Lakshmi. But then, keeping that wealth divine is just as important.

Chanakya talks about the concept of raja-rishi in the *Arthashastra*. A raja (king) who lives in the lap of luxury, but is also a philosopher (rishi). King Janak from the Ramayana, the father of Sita, was one such raja-rishi. Despite living a luxurious life, he was a wise and learned man.

Similarly, you can't judge a person's wealth from how much money they have. A poor person might be wealthier than you can imagine because of the sheer amount of wisdom he possesses.

Chanakya says that richness takes another form in our lives—friends. Mitra (friend) is an important part of building a good and strong kingdom. And the number of true friends by your side is nothing but a reflection of your strength and nobility.

Swami Chinmayananda put it in a nice manner. He said, 'It is friends who make you rich, not money.'

It would be a real achievement in your life if you could fulfil your desires, but also make a lot of friends in the process.

23

Ultimate Happiness

WHAT DOES ULTIMATE happiness mean?

It is a state where happiness is permanent.

It is the final purushartha (aim of life) after dharma, artha, kama—moksha.

Interestingly, Chanakya does not talk about moksha or give it any direct importance in the *Arthashastra*. It only comes up in *Chanakya Niti*, a different book written by him, for the common man.

According to Chanakya, if a king is too focused on moksha, he will not be able to fulfil his regular duties. He may get consumed by the highest spiritual activity and may lose focus of what is to be done in this world.

However, this does not mean Chanakya is completely dismissive of moksha. He believes that if one performs his duty as expected, moksha will be an automatic by-product. A life well-lived will inevitably lead you to moksha.

Chanakya says,

'He should devote himself equally to the three goals of life which are bound up with each other. For any of (the three viz.) spiritual good, material well-being and sensual pleasures, if excessively indulged in, does harm to itself as well as to the other two.' (1.7.4-5)

So for a person who is in a responsible position in life, it's advisable that he should focus only on the three primary goals of dharma, artha and kama. At the same time, there has to be a balance between the three aims. Because, as said above, the three are interconnected. They are dependent on each other.

So remember, if you are a householder, doing your duties itself is a path leading to moksha. So was with the king—having taken care of the kingdom and its administration naturally led him to moksha.

Now, in contrast, *Chanakya Niti* has another thought for the common man on the matter:

'Renounce one person for the sake of the family, a family for the sake of the village; the village for the sake of your country and even the [kingdom of] earth for one's own sake.'

A similar thought emerges in the Mahabharata too.

It talks about how every individual has a higher purpose in life. And that to attend to this higher purpose, he should be able to give up the minor challenges.

A family is made up of individuals. And the family is always more important than the individuals in it. The game is bigger than the player. So, at times, the individuals have to sacrifice their personal happiness for the greater good of the family.

Similarly, a village is made up of many families. So according to Chanakya, when it comes to the greater good of a village, a family should not be given priority.

Apply the same logic to a country.

But finally, there is something even above a country—your spiritual call. This higher calling is for your ultimate spiritual purpose of moksha. When such a call comes, you'll need to go beyond all worldly duties and responsibilities.

So here is how we should prepare for the highest spiritual calling:

Perform your worldly duties first

One should not use spiritual life as an escape from worldly duties. Those who run away from responsibilities can never succeed in spirituality. To put it simply, the spiritual world is not for the escapists.

Indeed, the spiritual path is for those who are resilient and unwavering in their dedication to getting better with each passing moment. So to enter spiritual life, you must fulfil your daily duties and worldly duties first.

Know that the world is not enough

Even if you are successful in this world, remember that it is not enough. There is always something more that can be achieved. The world is always making you a new offer. Are you listening?

So, even if you are the richest or the most powerful person

in the world, there are certain limitations that would apply to you, just as they would apply to any other human being. Remind yourself time and again that there is another world that you will have to eventually move towards—the spiritual world. Prepare yourself.

Take the leap of faith

There comes a time in life when you have to give up everything you have achieved.

It will be forcefully taken away from you. So, it is better to give it up with grace, rather than struggle at this point.

When such a time comes, one may wonder, 'Who will take care of me in the unknown spiritual world?' You will, at that time, take a leap of faith. Realize that finally, God takes care of everything.

When you take that ultimate call, you begin the final leg of your journey—a journey to discover yourself.

PROFESSIONAL LIFE

24

Going to the Workplace

THE CHAPTERS IN the previous section focused on how to apply Chanakya's teachings in one's personal life.

Here, from this chapter onwards, we will learn how to apply Chanakya's teachings in our professional life.

Remember, we're now moving from the 'individual' level to 'group dynamics'.

Part of this will obviously teach you how to deal with others as well. Because your success at the workplace is interlinked with the success of others at your workplace. This is a major shift in thinking that you need to partake of—from 'I' to 'we'.

So, let us begin.

Most of us work to make money. There is nothing wrong in that. But what is your purpose at your workplace? Do you feel inspired when you wake up every Monday morning? Do you say, 'Yes, I am looking forward to going to office today!'

If yes, then know that this excitement will ensure you have a great life ahead.

Chanakya says,

**'One should awaken and ponder over work to be done…
he should sit in consultation with councillors and
despatch secret agents…and then he should proceed to the
assembly hall…' (1.19.21-24)**

This is how a day should begin.

Chanakya has paved the way to prepare you for the day
ahead. One shouldn't just get up and rush to work.

The morning offers us a window to accomplish tasks in a
manner that no other time of the day does. So, do the most
important things in the morning itself.

The first step is to plan your day.

As soon as you wake up, after your prayers, ponder over
the work to be done during the day. It is not possible to always
complete everything in the morning. There are things still left
undone from the previous day, as well as new things that have
to be worked on today. So learn to prioritize.

Chanakya says that the king has to sit in consultation
with his councillors. The king had the privilege of having on
his call a group of experts who would report to him early in
the morning. This was so that before the day began, he was
well-informed about the happenings around his kingdom.

He could also send secret spies to gather information in
the morning so that he would get the necessary inputs for his
required work during the day.

So how do we apply this in our daily work? Here's how:

Be informed

It is very important to be aware of what is happening around you. The best way for you to stay up to date on the latest news is the newspaper. So when you enter your workplace, you can confidently participate in group discussions and sound well-informed.

Delegate

When you have multiple things to be done, the first and foremost thing is to decide who is going to do what. You don't need to accomplish *all* of your tasks. Some can be taken care of by juniors as well.

Let's assume you need an input from a junior for a board meeting you are going to have at noon. As soon as you start your work, call in a subordinate and delegate that work to him. Do this before 10 a.m. so he has enough time to research and find those inputs. Make sure to let him know he did well.

Finally, the key to a successful day is not to pack too many activities in one day. Remember to keep an hour free. Unexpected things may come up and you still want to be in a position to accommodate them in your daily schedule.

Most importantly, if there is some unfinished work despite your best efforts, remember that there is a tomorrow. Because it's essential that you start your day just as you end it—with a smile.

25

Silent Time

WORKPLACES TEND TO be noisy because regardless of how professional people are, offices are inevitably full of activity, with meetings and endless discussions happening even in open spaces.

In the midst of this chaos, how do we remain productive and efficient?

The only way out is to find your own space somewhere in the middle of this. And by space, I mean quiet time.

Silence is the only thing that allows us to contemplate, while also helping us rejuvenate ourselves in the process. Sitting quietly and mulling over things shouldn't be confused with laziness; this is the most productive hour of our day.

Think about it. If you continuously keep cutting the tree, when will you sharpen the saw? These moments of reflection with oneself are no different from finding time to 'sharpen the saw' until one is active again to deal with the new challenges of life.

But what would be the appropriate amount of silent time at the workplace?

The answer is, as much as possible. However, you cannot go about turning your office into a meditation centre! You have duties to perform after all. And spirituality should not be an excuse for laziness.

One day a person returned to work after attending a month-long meditation camp. He told his friend, 'I am going to meditate now in the other room, please take care of work.' The friend agreed and tried to support him initially.

But it soon became a problem. He was not able to complete his own work, let alone keep up with this 'meditating' friend's work.

One day this person asked his own guru for a solution. The guru said to him, 'Go and tell your friend, you meditate and I will do your work. But make sure your salary is also given to me.'

It's important to remember that the silent time being referred to is keeping in mind Chanakya's teachings. It is like recharging your mind, so that afterwards you feel ready for your next innings and can go at it with full force.

Chanakya said,

'In conformity with the place, time and work to be done, he should deliberate with one or two [persons], or alone by himself.' (1.15.41)

Here, Chanakya tells us about the relation between being with oneself and being more productive. In the above sutra he reveals the key to productive thinking—silence.

He says that firstly, one should come up with the right place and right time for thinking, as well as the work one needs to do. And then one should deliberate (think through) over all aspects of the issues in front of them, from all angles.

So let us see how we can use this time spent on deliberation to our benefit at our workplace:

Identify your work

We often don't even know what we're expected to do to fulfil our roles at work. And instead of addressing this crucial problem we continue to perform tasks without any guiding clarity.

Stop. Think clearly for a moment. This moment must precede any activity. Because no matter how fast you run, direction will always be more important than speed. It is better to be headed in the right direction than go to fast but nowhere.

So if you aren't sure of what is expected, it's best you stop and deliberate. For example, if you have been assigned a project, ask yourself—why has the project been given to me? What is the end result expected? Is there anyone else involved in the project? What are the deadlines?

Peter Drucker, the famous management guru, said, 'In today's world, work is not given, it is to be determined.'

Seek help

Once the task is clear, start planning its completion in detail.

Chanakya advises that we must go over our plans with an expert or two. This way, any doubts that remain even after asking your boss will be eliminated through your discussion with a friend or another senior person.

However, brainstorming only offers clarity when limited to a few people. Too many and that'll only lead to more confusion.

Go alone

In the long run, it is important to develop the habit of thinking all by oneself. In such moments of solitude, you will soon realize something amazing—when you develop the habit of clear thinking, you automatically develop intuitive thinking.

Intuitive thinking is the highest form of productivity. It allows you to foresee the future.

Peter Drucker doesn't seem to have said this. One of his articles is titled 'The Future That Has Already Happened' and the other thing he said is 'We cannot predict the future but we can invent it.'

Peter Drucker had once said, 'To see the future, that has happened.' At times, what we think will happen in the future has already happened. For example, we think our children will become smart in the future. But they are already smart now.

26

Eye on Accounts

IF YOU'RE ABLE to control your finances, then you're automatically in control of everything.

You may not agree with this but it's true. Let me explain.

Successful people invariably keep a track of their finances, because they understand the value of the money they have earned through hard work.

One of the important tools of finance is the accounting system.

Accounting is a process of recording all the financial transactions that have happened, especially helpful when running a large organization. This way, when we review any account statement, we have a comprehensive tool at our disposal to take the key decisions and catch any discrepancy.

Chanakya was an extremely clever person. He knew that keeping an eye on the accounts of a kingdom was one of the most important roles of a leader.

Therefore, he suggested keeping a track of accounts on

a daily basis,

'During the first eighth part of the day, he should listen to measures taken for defence and accounts of income and expenditure.' (1.19.9)

As the day began for a king, it was suggested that he be vigilant of the two most important aspects of his kingdom—the defence and the finances.

Chanakya mentions that the Danda (army) and Kosha (treasury) are the two most important pillars of a kingdom. Having a daily review of the two helps you stay in power.

Now, the most important word is 'listen'. Listen to the measures taken for defence and accounts. Whom did he want the king to listen to?

Obviously, the king was not going to take care of the defence and accounts all by himself. There were heads of both the departments who would be reporting to the king. They were the Senapati (head of the army) and the Kosha-adhyaksha (Finance head).

These two people were not ordinary. They were highly qualified and well-read, and also very worldly-wise. After all, they were among the best brains and advisors to the king itself.

Compare them to the modern-day national security advisor and the finance minister. These people give inputs to the president and the prime minister and help them take important national-level decisions. Such decisions not only impact the entire nation but their effects stay for generations to come.

So how do we follow this advice on keeping an eye on accounts in our workplaces?

Accounts is for all

It is a myth that accounts are only meant for the accounts department. These accounts should be reviewed by the leaders and every other employee connected with the organization. Apart from external bodies of governance like tax and regulatory bodies, these accounts can be accessed by every employee too.

We live in a world of transparency. All accounts are available as public documents. So remember, accounts are for all, including you and me.

Track on a daily basis

Whether at a personal or a professional level, make sure you keep a track of your accounts in terms of income and expenditure. A leader has to keep a watch on the incoming and outgoing.

Today there are management accounting systems available, specially designed to be less time-consuming and offering an overall view of where your company is at financially. A quick, one-minute glance is what a leader needs to get an idea of his financial status on a daily basis.

This can be followed by discussions on how to improve the financial health and the measures that need to be taken to do so. It could be a boost in sales or an increase in cash flow or even increasing the amount the company is choosing to invest.

Are you profitable?

Have you ever asked this question to yourself—am I a cost or a profit to the organization? When someone joins a company, he is given an appointment letter with a salary termed as cost to company (CTC).

But it is the responsibility of each person to make himself or herself profitable for the company. For example, if you are getting a salary of say, one lakh a month, and you are able to drive profits of say, one-and-a-half lakh, then you are an asset.

It does not matter if you are in sales or not. Each person should contribute in such a way that it adds to the profit of the company. Even a person from the HR department or production can think financially, track their accounts and make themselves and their department profitable.

Swami Chinmayananda put it well in the pledge he wanted his followers to take. He said, 'Giving more than what we take, and producing more than what we consume.'

This is the highest level of productivity.

27

Meeting People

HUMAN BEINGS CANNOT live or grow in isolation.

As a species, we are dependent on each other and are socially bound.

This is the reason why those who are less social, in other words 'introverts', are perceived as selfish or even 'weird'.

Similarly, even at workplaces, our ability to interact with others, get work done, lead people in the right direction, all determine the success we will enjoy in our careers.

Group discussions are part of the interviewing process for most jobs these days. Why? The objective is simple—to find out the efficacy of the interviewee's communication as well as their interpersonal skills.

Chanakya believed that regardless of where you stand on your communicative skills, one of the best ways to ensure that you're doing it right is to meet people. Regular interaction with successful people will help you keep things in perspective. At the same time, keeping yourself accessible to those who seek your aid will shape you out to be an accepted leader.

He says,

> **'Arriving in the assembly hall, he should allow**
> **unrestricted entrance to those wishing to see him in**
> **connection with their affairs.' (1.19.26)**

The raj darbar (assembly hall) was the place where the king met with others. And Chanakya suggested that the king give unrestricted access to those who wished to see him.

There were two kinds of assembly halls—'Diwane Aam' (assembly hall for everyone) and Diwane Khaas (assembly hall for special ones).

The first hall was where the king met the common man on a daily basis.

Chanakya insists that being directly in touch with people is an important aspect of leadership. And the king is bound to be approached by people with different objectives. But regardless of what they want, the king must have an open-door policy and always hear them out, be it opinions, complaints or simply a favour. And whatever the nature of their request, the king must take quick decisions and move forward. He should not keep any decisions pending.

The second hall was where the king met the advisors and experts, again on a daily basis. This involved meeting with wise people, who provided counsel and helped the king solve problems.

So the king's daily schedule was filled with various meetings, inputs from which were a source of his wisdom and helped ensure that he stayed vigilant.

So how should we go about holding meetings and of what kinds?

Formal meetings

The organization that you work for surely holds many formal meetings. Make sure you attend all of them. And walk in prepared for your meetings. If your presence is expected, do not take it casually, go well armed with all the information required of you. Always remember, it's better to be over-prepared.

Regardless of whether you are making a presentation, listen to others and take notes. Every meeting has the potential to open up your mind to various possibilities. So consider it as a learning opportunity.

My personal approach towards each meeting is to assume it's a class, and the presenter is a teacher who will teach me something new. Try this.

Informal meetings

Meetings need not always be formal in nature. Some happen in the canteen during lunch, or over a cup of coffee in a conference room. It could even happen as you are walking past your colleague's desk.

These informal chats are also essential. So keep your ears and eyes open even during these casual interactions with people.

One important suggestion I'd like to make—do not engage in gossip. Do not be the kind of person who is interested in the personal lives of others. Be a person who is genuinely concerned for others and simply wishes to keep himself updated on a regular basis.

Meetings led by you

There will be a time in your life when you'll be the one calling the shots. It's crucial that as a leader, you call your own meetings. They could be review meetings, or brainstorming sessions, or events of celebration.

Be a good organizer and make sure to make everyone feel included. Encourage everyone to participate. Engage with everyone, and listen to all viewpoints. Sometimes the best breakthrough ideas come from the last person, in the most unexpected manner.

A study of successful companies brought out surprising results—that the companies in which the senior management makes efforts to meet every last person in the organization and communicate with them are more respected than the ones that don't.

28

Managers Are Important

'I AM A self-made person.'

There cannot be a more arrogant and selfish statement than this.

People who say this do not value the contribution of others. A number of people help us become successful.

Some help us indirectly. Our parents, our teachers, our friends and workplace colleagues, all contribute to make us successful, but indirectly. Sometimes they become a hurdle to our progress. But by and large they are the reason why we stand on our feet and become successful in life. These people are the strong foundation of our lives.

A successful person was once asked, 'What is the secret of success?'

He answered, 'Success comes due to three factors—hard work, teamwork and God's grace.'

Now look at each of them separately. Yes, no one can become successful without putting in hard work. That is the starting point. One has to uplift oneself and take the first step.

But as the work grows, you will have to build a team. Then your team members will take up the task along with you, and it is the team's efforts that will take you ahead.

But are hard work and teamwork enough? No. It is God's grace that takes you to the finish line.

Chanakya, too, believes that the efforts of others are required for one to succeed.

Even a king could not succeed without good ministers. Chanakya says,

> 'Rulership can be successfully carried out (only) with the help of associates. One wheel alone does not turn. Therefore, he should appoint ministers and listen to their opinion.' (1.7.9)

The relation between a king and his minister was like that between the sea and waves. Both were dependent on each other, influenced by, and influencing, each other.

Chanakya says that one should have many associates so that the work can be carried out successfully. They are an extension of you. If you do not have one, start appointing them.

I have personally seen company owners who do not trust anyone at all. When it comes to their business, they restrict all control to themselves.

Even if they have a manager, it is only as a formality. They do not allow the manager to think, innovate or contribute. Such business leaders like to have yes-men around them and follow the 'no questions asked' policy.

It makes for poor leadership skills.

Chanakya advises that the ministers should be contributors, and the king should listen to them.

So, how do you get work done in your workplace with reference to Chanakya's advice?

Right person for the right job

When you appoint someone, you need to ask yourself a few important questions. Is the person whom I am appointing fit for the job? Does s/he have the required skill set and experience? Is he the right person to be delegated this work?

If the person has no experience, you will have to train him. Is he trainable?

Look at the natural strengths of the person and based on that, make the person a part of your project.

Pay well

Pay the person well. Pay as high as you can afford. Today, human capital is the best investment you can make. Invest in your people. Train them and mentor them, and they become your biggest assets (capital).

A leader who commanded a large police force once said, 'I take care of them, and they take care of my work.' So once you take care of the financial concerns of your team members, they will be mentally free to perform. They will be able to focus more on the job.

Motivate them

Payment is not the only thing that keeps a person going. Keep motivating your managers. Empower them. Let them take decisions. Allow them to fail. All this is part of growth.

No one becomes an expert on day one. It is years of trial and error that finally help you arrive at a point where you understand what works and what does not. It is your duty to train your managers and subordinates and give them the benefit of your experience too.

Give them pep talks, take them out for a dinner or a picnic. Involve them, educate them. Sometimes the best motivation could be even a pat on the shoulder, a thank-you, or even a sorry.

Give credit

Finally, do not forget this—give them credit for your success.

It is said that you will be happy if you work hard and succeed, regardless of who takes the credit.

Our former president, Dr A.P.J. Abdul Kalam, was known for this quality. When any of his projects succeeded, he gave the credit to his team members and project managers. When he failed, he took full responsibility for the failure.

When we practise this, we develop another quality of leadership, the one which is the most important—humility.

Humility is what draws everyone towards you.

When you have humility and a sense of gratitude, everything falls in place for you to succeed.

29

Creating Your Workplace

It is fun.

It is creative.

It is fulfilling.

I'm talking about the space you work in! Have you ever got an opportunity to create your own workplace? Whether it's a factory, or an office or even your own desk, it is important to create your own workplace.

It is a misconception that your company owner or the architect creates the workplace for you. Even if they have set it up in the past, it is your responsibility to customize it and make it your own. After all, your workspace and the way you manage it reflects your character.

There are two types of workplaces that can be created—one is called green-field project and the other, brown-field project. The green-field involves starting from scratch. So you have the freedom to use your imagination and creativity to design the space as you want.

However, in the brown-field project, your workplace already exists and is already operational on your arrival. What you can do in this case though is upgrade that space, change it in ways and make it unique.

What advice did Chanakya give to create a new place?

'On a site recommended by experts in building, he should cause the royal residence to be built, with a rampart, a moat and gates and provided with many halls.' (1.19.1)

Imagine a situation where you have been appointed to set-up a company's workspace from scratch. A large piece of land is given to you and you have to create everything. And you have full freedom to do it the way you want.

Here, Chanakya says that such a place should be recommended by experts who have technical knowledge about building and construction. There are many experts who play different roles in this case. The environmentalists who will tell you if the place is ideally located in terms of weather and let you know ways of lessening any damaging impact the construction might have on the surrounding areas. Similarly, the architect, the vastu pundits, etc. will consult you on the various things you need to keep in mind before you go ahead with the project.

And then you start looking at what is required as per your work and responsibilities. So, in this case the king is building a fort. He has to think through on aspects like security, residences, halls and other important features of the fort.

Similarly, we too need to create our workplaces with careful planning.

The infrastructure you create for your workplace has to be an inspiring one. Remember, most of us spend more time in our offices than in our homes. So, such a place where you spend most of your time should have a positive impact on your mind.

So how should you go about it? Here are some tips based on Chanakya's teachings:

Begin small

I am not suggesting that everyone gets the opportunity to build a massive architectural structure. But you must try to make whatever is given to you more beautiful.

Let us assume you have been appointed to a new office. The day you join, you will be given a desk and area to work in. That itself is the right place to begin with.

Observe the space to see how the previous person working in that space maintained it. Now, check out the provisions already available. Keep the good useful things, and then change the remaining for the better. Your desk can be altered as per your requirement and comfort. Where are you going to keep your laptop, papers, etc.? Is there a pin-up board for pinning up quotes and reminders?

Take these things into consideration and accordingly get some stationery for your desk. Also keep flowers on your desk, or hang a beautiful painting around to give it an aesthetic feel. These are small things that will go a long way.

Big opportunity

As time progresses, bigger opportunities will come your way.

Suddenly one day, you may be called by the management and told to head a department or even take charge of a completely new office. Here, you get the chance to change not just your desk, but the workplace of your whole team.

This is the time to, as Chanakya says, get hold of the experts. Listen to them carefully. But remember, you will also have to list down your own expectations and share the same with the experts. Only then will you get better inputs from them. A designer can work on a design only if he knows exactly what his client wants.

Involve other team members

I remember a company where a person got promoted to head a department. He was given the freedom to design the whole department. He immediately called his juniors and asked for their inputs and had these very inputs incorporated. This was a very good move on his part as it sent the right message to the team members—that they count.

Thus, to make the workplace productive, make sure you take into account each team member's opinion.

Leave such a mark on your workplace that the people who follow your steps should feel proud that they are following a legend.

30

Training People

LIFE IS NOTHING but a quest for knowledge. First we learn from others. Then we impart that knowledge to others.

Look at our life itself—in the first stage of our life we are trained by our parents and teachers. Then, we practise what we learned from them throughout our lives. And then finally, towards the latter stage of our life, we start training others, be it in our personal life (teaching our children and grandchildren) or professional life (teaching our subordinates at work).

This is how experience and knowledge flows on from one generation to the next.

In an address to the Indian civil servants, Prime Minister Narendra Modi mentioned about 'institutional memory' being documented. He said that each civil servant is a leader. They have done transformational work in their own postings. Now, before they retire, they should pass on their wisdom and experience to others.

This is the kind of training required for an individual, a

company and a nation to grow.

Chanakya also emphasized this kind of approach when he said,

'He (king) should strive to give training to the prince.'
(5.6.39)

Excellence is impossible without training.

Chanakya insists that the king (leader) has to make sure the prince (future leader) is trained.

The key word here is 'strive'. What he means is that one has to go out of one's way and put in that extra effort to train others.

Training should not be considered a part-time activity. It is part of anyone's main job, for it is the very foundation of success.

Look at any field—sports, arts, business, literature—all successful people in any field were trained by experts. So, if you want productive people in your offices, make sure you give the utmost importance to training.

Here is how you go about it:

Create a training culture

Most organizations have a department dedicated to training. But somehow, it is not given its due worth. In multinational companies, it is usually the Human Resources (HR) department that takes the responsibility of organizing and conducting training programmes. They generally design the programme, plan training schedules, keep everyone in the loop and carry out the training programme. This is fine.

But Chanakya offers a better insight with inputs that would enhance the training programmes in your company. He says that the king should 'strive' to give training. As a leader, are you giving topmost importance to training? You must do so, because your attitude towards training will reflect in your interactions all too clearly. Only when you take them seriously yourself will the training programmes be treated seriously by others. Otherwise, they will turn into just another picnic or break sponsored by the company.

Be a trainer yourself

Now, this is the key. A leader should not just tell others to conduct and attend training programmes; he should *become* a trainer. This does not mean that all the training programmes should be conducted by the leader himself. It means that the leader should at least get involved in a deeper, more hands-on manner than just sanctioning a budget.

You can show your involvement by providing some key inputs in designing the training programmes. At least dedicate one week a year to conducting a training programme yourself. Share your vision during one of those sessions. Inspire those around you. Tell them what you have done, and what the company is planning to do.

This sends a strong message to everyone in the company. Lead by example.

Train the trainers

Sometimes the sheer number of employees in the company makes it impossible for a leader to meet everyone individually.

So how does one reach out to every last person in the organization? And this is more complicated by the fact that offices these days are spread across cities and even countries.

It is possible. To tackle this challenge all you need to do is train others under you. Impart your vision and leadership skills onto others. As a leader you will thus create more leaders.

It is far more efficient if ten others are collectively saying what you have been trying to convey all by yourself. This also perpetuates your legacy. Sure, others may have different styles of saying the same thing. But remember, once you've shared your vision with them, you've completed half your mission.

Make it a learning organization

Encourage each person to be a teacher in his own way. Even an office boy can become a good teacher, for it is he who will train the next office boy. A good administrator should 'strive' to create good administrators out of the future generations.

It is never about the budget or finances available for training. It is finally all about your attitude towards training, and the importance given to it. When you show employees that they too can impart the knowledge they have gained along the way, you empower them to become independent thinkers.

But start with yourself. When are you conducting the first training for the juniors in your team?

Let the teacher in you speak.

31

Two Keys to Success

THIS CHAPTER TALKS about the two keys to success—the treasury and the army.

Growth is a natural process. But it can also be strategically planned.

Just look at a forest and a farm. Both are part of nature. They are equally subject to natural laws. But the difference is that a forest grows of its own accord, while a farm is designed by humans.

In both the cases, plants and trees grow in them. But the farm yields crops because the farmer does a lot of planning, ploughs, plants the right seed, waters it regularly and patiently waits for his efforts to bear fruition.

In the similar way, our professional life too has two methods in which it grows. One involves no intervention, and the other involves careful planning to steer it in the right direction.

Some people grow in their careers just by working in one

company all their lives. They get promoted simply because of their seniority in the organization. In such a case, all it takes is for a senior person to leave the organization, and this person effortlessly replaces him or her. In such a case, little or no importance is placed on performance evaluation. This kind of career growth is clearly not a strategic one.

But there are people who, much like farmers, think through and chalk out a career path. They pursue courses that help them acquire the skill set suitable for their career. They consult others and then slowly and surely move in that direction, towards a planned route to success.

We all know Chanakya to be a 'kingmaker'. He believed that the position of a leader did not just 'happen'. There is an entire thought process involved—the selection of the right person, the training given, the regular checks and finally a guide to direct the leadership—a mentor to the leader, who will be help in all situations and challenges the leader faces.

So, what is the key to successful leadership?

Chanakya says,

'The king brings under his sway his own party as well as the party of the enemies, by the (use of the) treasury and the army.' (1.4.2)

The two keys to success is right use of the 'treasury' and the 'army'.

Here, Chanakya explains that the leader should bring under his influence, power or command, his own people and also of the enemies, by the right use of the treasury and the army. This means he will be in total control of his own people (citizens) and also in control of his enemies.

These are the eternal principles of leadership. Treasury stands for finances. And the army isn't just the armed forces, rather, it means the strength of the masses.

Let us have a close look at how we can use Chanakya's mantra in our corporate world:

The Finance and HR

Every good leader knows that the success of his business largely depends on two people—the finance head and the HR head. The finance head would typically be the CFO (Chief Financial Officer) while the Human Resources (HR) head would focus on the issues faced by the employees of the company.

Planning a project

Chanakya's principle can be applied to assignments we take up in our workplaces. While planning a project, think of these two areas—what is the finance involved (treasury) and who are the people involved (army).

Once you have a clear understanding of what it will cost you and who are the right people for the project, your plan is bound to succeed. Because really, these are the two main concerns.

So for example, say you are organizing a picnic for the company, or a marketing campaign. Just check up on these two things. Draw a budget, and make sure the right person is in charge of the whole activity. With these two major things sorted out, everything will fall in place.

Next leader

When you want to grow in your career, remember this lesson from Chanakya. As you get promoted, you need to find a suitable person who will take care of your current responsibilities.

As I climb up the ladder, which of my colleagues deserves to take up my current role? While you may have many options, Chanakya's teaching helps you arrive at a conclusion.

Your next leader should be the one who can understand finance (treasury) and also has good people skills (army). You should promote such a person to take up your position and provide them the required training.

Keep learning and growing in the field of finance and people-management skills.

This is a lifelong process for your career growth.

32

Decision-making

THE RIGHT DECISION at the right time can change our destiny forever.

Decisions, big and small, can have lasting, irreversible impact on our lives, careers, and even relationships. The courses we choose in college, the job we choose, the person we decide to spend the rest of our life with—all these decisions will remain with us forever.

Decision-making is a skill, a knack, an art. The good news is that one can become better and better in taking the right decisions.

Your life's success and failure both depend a lot on your efficiency in making decisions.

One day a successful business leader was asked, 'What is the secret of success?' He said, 'Taking the right decisions.' He was asked again, 'How does one take the right decisions?' Pat came the reply, 'By taking wrong decisions.'

Chanakya had trained people not only to take decisions

but take them quickly.

He said,

'He should hear (at once) every urgent matter, (and) not put it off. An (affair) postponed becomes difficult to settle or even impossible to settle.' (1.19.30)

Therefore, this sutra talks about various factors that go into the decision-making process.

Whenever a person approaches the leader with any urgent matter, the leader should not postpone it. In case the decision or matter is postponed, it may later become impossible to manage.

For example, if the person comes to warn him of a fire, and the leader does not pay heed to the person, the situation will definitely become worse.

Let us look in detail at what Chanakya has suggested we do while taking decisions:

Hear

This is the defining quality of a great leader—the ability to listen. People are always talking and as they speak, they articulate their opinions, suggestions, remarks, among other things. A lot of the person reflects in the words he chooses to utter. But are we listening? Mostly not. This partly has something to do with the fact that we don't receive formal training in listening properly. This isn't exactly considered a 'skill' to be taught. But you must take it into account very seriously.

It is not necessary that everything people say is right.

Nevertheless, it is important to listen to them and gather information to use for your own critical thinking (anvikshiki). This method has been given its due importance in the training of the prince in the very first chapter of the *Arthashastra*, named 'Anvikshiki', where Chanakya teaches the leaders to think logically and take important decisions.

Equal importance

Do not take anything for granted. Every matter, regardless of its urgency, has to be heard patiently. For a leader, no matter is less important than the other.

So, sometimes you may come across a matter that doesn't concern you at all but is of utmost urgency to someone else. You must give this person a chance to voice his or her thoughts. Listen even if you don't have solutions to offer because sometimes the best solution may lie in the very act of lending an ear to the person.

Please note that at such times people might articulate themselves in an abstract manner, they may not necessarily say what they mean. When a person says, 'I am tired,' he doesn't just mean tired at a physical level. He could be mentally exhausted too. There could be other, bigger reasons why he is tired. It could be a long day at office, or a long journey, or fatigue that has happened due to some sports activity. Try to understand the crux of the matter.

Don't postpone

Having listened to the person's problem, you have to take the next step. And it's crucial that you respond, not react.

What if you just keep quiet and do nothing? Well, then the matter remains pending and it's exactly what Chanakya advises against. Also, the more such small decisions pile up, the more impossible it becomes to clear them up later.

So remember to complete your work on a daily basis. Do not keep decisions pending, unless they require any inputs from others. Even in that case, take a decision as soon as you get the input you seek.

Once you are in full control of yourself, you will achieve the highest level of productivity at your workplace.

33

Role Clarity

WHAT AM I doing?

Why am I doing this?

What is the purpose of my work?

These aren't ordinary questions, for the answers to these can redefine our perception of the self, can change the very course of our lives.

In the corporate world, most of us hesitate to ask our superiors these questions. We usually just get to our work without much thought. Whatever project is handed to us, we go ahead and do it. But despite accomplishing our tasks, the end of each day brings with it a sense of dejection....one that haunts us till the next day.

But wait, it gets more interesting. The more efficient and productive you are, the more work they pile on you.

Chanakya mentioned in the *Arthashastra* that if we want to succeed as a leader, we must first seek clarity in our roles. He said,

'From the capacity for doing work is the ability of the person judged. And in accordance with the ability, by suitably distributing rank among ministers and assigning place, time and work to them, he should appoint all the ministers.' (1.8.28-29)

To put it simply, don't be confused. And do not confuse others.

As a leader, it is important to have and give 'role clarity' to others. So, when delegating work to others, pause for a moment and consider what Chanakya says—are you delegating work according to the capacity of the person? Are you giving it at the right place and time? Should you even be delegating this work?

Here are some simple steps to make sure you're following these precepts:

What is the work

While delegating the work, be clear about what the work entails in the first place. Answer the question, 'What is the work to be done?' Once you know exactly what needs to be done, you can share that clarity with others around you. This will only help ensure that the work is completed efficiently and without any confusion.

And this applies to small tasks as well. What is the objective to be achieved? Who will be impacted? What is the overall purpose? Is it to be done at all?

Who is the person

Never delegate a task on an impulse. You need to first think of the right person for the job. Is there someone in your team who can do it? Does s/he have the ability to deliver what's required and do it within the deadline? If there is no one in the team, then perhaps you should even consider hiring someone to do it.

At times while delegating it becomes important to consider outsourcing the work to an external agency. Because even if it costs you a bit, it will be time-effective.

Empower the person

Once you have decided who the right person is for the job, you must empower them so they can perform well. If need be, train the person and give guidance from time to time.

While doing all this, remember not to micro-manage. You need to trust them to do the work properly. Yes, your job is to monitor, review and supervise the work. But do just that. Only empowered people feel responsible. Take away their empowerment and you might be looking at shoddy results.

The chairman of E Stars, Rajesh Doshi, once said about managing multiple projects, 'I think through the whole project in my head first, select the right person next, give the vision and role clarity. And then sit back and watch the whole thing grow.'

34

Walk Around

THERE IS A story about a Japanese company.

One day the chairman of this company was sitting in his office. They owned a manufacturing plant and he wanted some details about it from one of the department heads there.

He called his office, but it was answered by another person. The person informed the chairman, 'The plant head is on the floor with his workers.'

The chairman said, 'Tell him to call back when he is done with his work.' It took about two hours for the department's head to return the chairman's call.

Now imagine this situation, but in the context of an Indian company. In most of the companies in India, when the chairman calls, the department's head is expected to take the call immediately. If not, then he's expected to call back right away once he's been informed of the chairman's call.

This is the difference in our working cultures. The Japanese know that spending time on the floor with workers is most important for the plant or factory's manager. While sitting in the office is considered normal for a plant manager in India.

Also, being made to wait for two hours would be treated with respect in Japan, as the plant manager is showing dedication towards his work.

So, the message is that even if you have an office, it is important to not just sit at your table or desk, but walk around and take a look at what happens on the floor. This helps you stay in touch with the ground realities of your workplace.

Chanakya had given a similar advice to the king too:

> **'During the seventh part of the day, he should review elephants, horses, chariots and troops.' (1.19.15)**

Usually, our mental image of a king working involves him sitting on a throne and giving orders. But Chanakya's daily plan for the king involved him spending a major part of his time working *outside* his assembly hall.

The king was suggested to walk around for an hour and a half every day. Army being a major component of a king's strength, he was told to review the condition of his elephants, horses, chariots and troops. This ensured that he did not take things lightly as far as his troops were concerned.

In the structural design of a kingdom, the army was placed on the outskirts. Some troops might be close to the king, but majorly they were away from the main palace, guarding the borders.

So a king was supposed to physically go and keep a tab on his entire army, including the animals also.

What does it indicate to us? It means that we should not

be sitting at the 'palace' (in our case, our office desks), but instead take a reality check on a daily basis.

There are many benefits we will derive if we take a walk around our workplaces on a regular basis. Here are a few:

It is an exercise

It is very boring and monotonous to just sit at one place and work on the computer all day. It's actually not good for your body or mind. So a short walk around your office from time to time will make you feel better. It will give you the much-needed break from monotony, and will also help the blood circulation in your body.

After all, walking around is an exercise in itself. It is suggested that after every one-and-a-half hours, one should take a walking break. Even a few stretching exercises are recommended. Yoga teachers even suggest some easy deep breathing exercises that one can practise at work.

Trust, but...

It is good to trust your colleagues. But it is not good to trust them too much. Many people who sit in offices feel that once the work is delegated, their work is over. They can trust their subordinates to finish the job.

But remember, that is a wrong mindset. Trust your people, but not completely. There are various examples where people's trust has been totally broken by the ones they trusted the most. A quick walk around will help you keep a check on what your subordinates are doing and might even reveal some useful information.

Surprise checks

During the daily walk, do a surprise check on your team members. Just check what they are doing on their computers. Observe the papers lying around on their tables. Ask them a few questions at their desks.

This will keep them alert. Being supervised is an essential part of not taking your job for granted.

Also, by walking around you can solve many problems. Just going to their work areas and having a small discussion with them will provide the inputs you need to find the areas of your work that need improvement.

So walk around daily and see yourself grow in your professional life.

35

Habit of Documentation

READING BUILDS THE character of a man. Writing completes it.

This sums up the knowledge and experience of a person in full measure. In life, if we follow this principle we can work wonders.

When we read, we're soaking in the knowledge of another person. It helps to learn from their experiences. While a well-read person has learnt a lot from others, he also has a lot of his own personal experiences. Such a person should pen his or her experiences down.

Such a life documented in any manner can inspire generations to come.

Apart from recording our experiences, writing helps us find the underlying coherence in our thoughts.

Therefore, to become successful in life it is essential to start documenting and keeping records of all that one does.

Chanakya was one such great person.

He read everything that the previous teachers of the *Arthashastra* wrote and equipped himself well with knowledge of the past. But he did not stop at that alone. Armed with all that wisdom, he built an empire under the rulership of his able student Chandragupta Maurya.

Now, after creating the golden era of India, during those days, Chanakya wrote his own *Arthashastra*—a documentation of his lifelong experiences.

Imagine, what if Chanakya was only well read, but did not write the *Arthashastra*? Then all his wisdom would have been lost forever. I would not have written this book. You would never have read it.

We should all be grateful to Chanakya. I personally cannot thank him enough for writing his wonderful thesis of *Arthashastra*—a book that has become a source of inspiration for leaders in every field from across the globe.

Chanakya himself says about reading and writing,

'This single treatise on the science of politics (Kautilya's *Arthashastra*) has been prepared mostly by bringing together the teachings of as many treatises on the science of politics (previous *Arthashastras*) as have been composed by ancient teachers for the acquisition and protection of the earth.' (1.1.1)

This is the opening verse of the *Arthashastra*. Chanakya shares the whole background behind how he wrote his own *Arthashastra*.

He says he prepared this work based on a study of teachings by previous scholars. And his objective of writing this is to protect the earth. How? In simple terms, by learning how to rule a kingdom effectively.

Here's what we can learn from Chanakya on this matter:

Daily habit

Writing should become a daily habit.

When we think of the word 'writing', the first images that come to mind are those of huge books and reports. One should not think like that. Writing doesn't have to be a herculean task. You can start in a small way, like making a to-do list on a daily basis or keeping a dairy.

Unfortunately, the only training in writing given to us in our current education system is to prepare for exams. But we need to develop it further. We should start writing as a no-brain activity, an activity that does not require too much mental effort on our part. For example, if a person drives his car every day to office on the same route, after a point it becomes an effortless no-brain activity.

At the workplace

Most offices do not train people in the habit of writing and documentation at an individual level. Try the habit of writing and document the work done at your office.

For example, when you go for a meeting, carry a pen and pad. Make detailed notes. When you do that your mind captures more and you are more attentive. So by the end of the meeting, you have all the points that have been addressed on paper. You have a ready list of tasks that need to be performed by you.

Even when you are thinking about your work, think on

paper. Write down as you ideate. It helps to develop and expand those ideas further.

Refine it

Your first notes may not be perfect. Usually, they aren't. If they have to be presented to someone, you will have to refine them further. Even in school we had a rough notebook and then the final notebook, remember?

Similarly, when you write, try and refine your writing even further. There are various tips available on the Internet on how to write better. Take the initiative to look those up. Take a few courses on how to document your office work. It will help in the long run.

Leave a legacy

The habit of documentation is about leaving a legacy behind. Your notes, books and research papers become reference points for others.

Do not think about who your audience is when you sit down to write. You will one day be surprised when someone somewhere will pick up an idea from your book and take it forward.

After all, this is how history is created.

36

Your Contacts

'YOUR CONTACTS BECOME your contracts.'

This was said by a sales manager who was addressing a group of new recruits in a company.

He was stating an eternal truth which can not only help achieve success in sales, but also in life itself. In short, your relationships with others help you succeed in your professional life.

The human mind is a strange thing. If it wants to do something it will accomplish the task, come what may. Therefore, here lies the trick for success—first build your relations. Work will get done automatically. Chanakya was a master strategist in this matter.

Relationships were top priority for him.

This is the advice he gives,

'He should establish contacts with forest chieftains, frontier chiefs and chief officials in the cities and the countryside.' (1.16.7)

One should build contacts everywhere.

When a king is running a kingdom, he has to deal with the common man as well as other leaders like himself. This is where Chanakya's advice is to be taken.

What kind of contacts did Chanakya suggest the king should make?

Forest chief: A king might have been all-powerful sitting in his palace. But in the forest, the forest chief was the leader of the tribal people who lived there. If the king failed to build a relationship with the forest chief, he might not even have got an entry into the forest. His power then would be of no use there.

Frontier chiefs: There were many villages bordering the country. The frontier chiefs of these borders held crucial information about activities across the border. So the king would have been smart to build relationships with them, as their knowledge could help him defeat the enemy across the border.

Chief officials in cities: They were powerful people. They controlled the economy of the city. These chief officials were like the IAS officers who are collectors and commissioners of various departments. They didn't just work for the king, but were also the ones who carried out all the projects for the leader. So having a good rapport with them allowed the king to have more control over his kingdom, even at a local level.

Chief officials in countryside: Like the chief officials in the cities, there were powerful government officials in rural areas too. They had a deep understanding of what went on in the villages. So again, it was rather wise if the king was on good terms with such officials.

Now, how do we apply the advice mentioned above to our workplaces?

Contacts in your office

First and foremost, you should develop contacts within your workplace itself. You will have to interact with your colleagues on a regular basis to get your work done. So a healthy relationship with coworkers is something Chanakya would encourage.

But do not make the relations at your workplace only transactional. Have a more human-centric approach. Wish them on their birthdays, send a thank-you note. Drop in or invite them for a cup of coffee or a lunch. If possible, try a home visit too. They will be pleasantly surprised.

Contacts in associations

Each of us works not just in a company or an organization. We actually work in an industry. For example, if you work in a school as a teacher, you're not just part of the school but also the education system as a whole.

Similarly, each workplace is part of a bigger universe. Therefore, there are associations where such professionals come together. Say the Printers' Association of India, the Publishers' Association, School Principals' Associations, Marketing and Branding Associations, etc. All these platforms expose these professionals to the universe of those who are doing the same job as them, only elsewhere. And this serves to open their minds and helps them learn from each other.

These are larger communities. Try and go for their meetings. Become a member. Attend training programmes and conferences. You will develop contacts in your professional field which could prove to be very useful in the long run.

Contacts with clients

Many people think customer care is only related to the sales or marketing departments. As an organization, one has to be aware that each one of us is now part of the larger industry.

We earn the respect of our clients by the way we treat them during as well as after business hours. Again, remember not to make it only work-related. Build relationships.

Other than this, there are small things you can do to start making contacts. Join a like-minded WhatsApp group. Don't just send forward messages; call them. Meet them one on one or during group meetings. Join your school alumni group. There are friends you will reconnect with. Don't just sit at home. Walk into your next-door neighbour's house and say a 'hello'.

As Swami Chinmayananda put it well, 'To have friends, be a friendly person first.'

37

Contracts

IN THE PREVIOUS chapters we understood the importance of writing and taking notes. We learned how documentation helps us save our experience and knowledge and pass it on to the future generations.

In this chapter, we take a look at documentation again, but in a different aspect. Specifically, writing and signing contracts.

Contracts are present in pretty much every aspect of life today. When we join a company, we sign a contract. When we buy a house, rent a property, employ someone, have a vendor agreement, all these actions are legally bound by contracts.

So what exactly is a contract? It is a legal agreement between two people, or parties, where certain terms and conditions agreed upon are put down on paper, signed by the parties involved, along with witnesses, and is considered legally binding. Any deviations from such a contract can be challenged in court.

Centuries ago, Chanakya, much ahead of his time, gave us guidance on how to draw up a contract. He says,

'One should make a deal, with one's own people or with strangers, in the presence of a witness, in an open manner, properly declaring it with respect to place, time, quantity and quality.' (3.12.53)

Chanakya is meticulous in his approach to making a contract.

He includes the various aspects one must take into consideration while making a deal. He suggests that a deal should be made with clear understanding, regardless of whether it is with one's own relative or friend, or a total stranger.

What you have agreed upon has to put down in writing. Also, he says you must do this in front of witnesses. This way neither parties involved can turn back on what they agreed upon in the long run. The deal must be made in an open manner in order to maintain complete transparency.

Both parties should clearly decide and agree on the deliverables, whatever they may be. Each party should be clear on what they must give and take to avoid confusion and misunderstanding in future. This is called service-level agreements.

So what are the suggestions given by Chanakya that we can apply in our daily lives?

Have clarity first

When you are about to take up some work, be clear on what your roles and responsibilities are. If you are joining a company, be clear on what's expected of you, as well as what your expectations are. Suppose you are appointed as a manger of a division, discuss in detail what are your job profile entails.

Even if you are joining a company owned by a family member, do not take it for granted. Have an elaborate discussion on your role in the company to avoid confusion in future.

Agree on paper

Go on to the next level. What you have discussed and agreed upon, put it down on paper.

Don't make a contract first and then discuss. It should be the other way round. Discuss first and then make a contract. I am not suggesting that all agreements have to be prepared legally. Not every contract requires a a lawyer to draft it. If it's a big company contract, then yes, it requires a legal person to draft it. But for small things just make a few notes and come to an agreement. Make sure both of you read it carefully. If there is any counterview, discuss and debate it.

Focus on the work

Now, once that is done, forget the contract. Just keep it in a file safely for future reference. You can also scan a copy and mail it to yourself as a soft copy for record-keeping.

Now that the contract is signed, focus on the deliverables. Focus on the work and its completion. The real success is not just in signing the perfect contract, but in achieving the targets.

Finally, the role of a contract is to provide clarity.

On a daily basis

Make it a daily habit to put things on record. Practise it in your workplace. If you speak to someone and agree on doing some work, just put it on paper or in an email. This way everyone's clear on what is to be expected. Now don't just develop this habit of recording the agreement, but also remember that giving quality output is your top priority.

It is always better to under-promise and over-deliver. So try to surpass the expectations you set or agreed upon. Go that extra mile. It is what will set you apart from the rest.

38

Work-related Travel

YOUR WORK MAY not involve travelling.

But most of you will have to commute to work on a daily basis.

For people in certain departments like sales and marketing, travel is part of their job. In fact, if a salesperson is sitting in his or her office, s/he is considered unproductive. So for such people travelling is very much required.

But here I am specifically talking about people who need to plan their travel as far as work is concerned. Even if yours is a desk job at one office location, you need to plan your commute to work.

In fact, any business travel in general has to be planned carefully.

Chanakya gives a tip for the same,

'He should start after making proper arrangements for vehicles, draught animals and retinue of servants.' (1.16.5)

Planning is key to success. 'The more we sweat during peace time, the less we bleed during wartime', goes the famous army saying.

Chanakya was a meticulous planner himself and believed in being over-prepared. He advised the king to make proper arrangements of vehicles before travelling. Because vehicles have to be in a good condition and well-equipped for the complete journey, it is crucial that the king have his vehicle properly checked for a long journey.

Now Chanakya also takes into consideration the group of attendants or servants required as part of the support system in the king's convoy. With the seasons and unpredictable terrain of the journey, Chanakya takes into account everything that would determine the journey a success.

Let us see how these travel tips by Chanakya can be applied in our time:

Plan before you start

Most of us travel to our workplaces on a daily basis. If you plan your to-and-fro travel carefully, you will have a very productive time, both at office and also at home.

Suppose a lady has to reach her office by 9 a.m. She will have to manage the early morning household work and then get to work on time as well. In such a case, careful planning on the previous day itself helps. She can be prepared in advance and her morning will be smooth sailing.

So with a little bit of time-management skills, she can leave stress-free to catch her bus or train.

Plan your travel

It is normal to reach office late because of traffic jams. But this can easily be avoided with some planning in advance. One cannot avoid traffic on roads, but one can avoid traffic hours altogether. The pattern of peak hours is not hard to guess at all. They are generally during the morning and evening hours before the office starts and after the workday ends.

If you know the pattern, then plan accordingly. Avoid roads that usually suffer from traffic jams; instead, look for alternative routes. You can also leave a little early. If you have your own car, use Google Maps to avoid routes with traffic jams.

I know of a lady who reaches her office half an hour early and completes most of her important tasks before others arrive. She is so efficient that she has an arrangement with her boss to leave half an hour early to avoid the evening traffic hours too!

Outstation travel

This can also be made easy. Try to plan all your outstation travel a few days or preferably, weeks in advance. Check what is the purpose of the meeting and who else is required from your team for the meeting. Inform and take an appointment in advance with the other person whom you are meeting. Then book your tickets, accommodation, etc.

If you're travelling to a new city, have a local guide or driver who will help you reach the venue of the meeting before time, someone who knows the roads and the traffic patterns well.

Finally, apart from work, make sure you have some spare time to go to some important tourist destinations, do a little bit of shopping for yourself, friends and family.

Most importantly, try the local cuisine. Every place has something unique to offer.

Upon returning, you'll have so many stories to share. You will come back richer and happier.

And that is what travel should do.

39

From Yearly Planning to a Daily Review

SET A GOAL.

Then go ahead and achieve it.

This is not an impulsive statement. It is actually a serious exercise. It is a commitment. And Chanakya would bring in strategy to achieve it.

Many do not know how to set a goal. They lead monotonous, purposeless lives. Therefore, to change your life you need to first set a goal. There are many goal-setting exercises and workshops being conducted by trainers.

Even companies and organizations have goal-setting activities these days. These involve serious discussions with the chairman, senior management and the execution team.

Once the goal is set, the next step is to build a strategy around it. And then its execution.

But the key to success is not just setting the goal and

working on it. The most important part is to review it on a regular basis.

There is an age-old formula used by Chanakya on yearly planning and daily review. It is a wonderful model being implemented by some of the greatest organizations today. However, many of them are not aware that this is a strategy developed by Chanakya centuries ago.

Let us look at what Chanakya would say as far as financial goals are concerned. He said,

'He should check the accounts for each day; group of five days (weekly), fortnight; month, four months and a year.'
(2.7.30)

The king was supposed to be constantly alert. He had to keep a check on any developments in his kingdom on a regular basis. The above sutra by Chanakya is giving the king a direction as to how he needs to go about reviewing the accounts.

A timely and periodic review will always be helpful.

The thing is, once we start implementing our plan we inevitably face problems one after another. So when the leader takes the initiative to review it, the people in his team stay alert, leaving them no room to give an excuse for unaccomplished goals at the end of the year.

Let us see how to plan our work using this framework:

Set a goal

As mentioned earlier, it is important to set a goal. That is the first step. So if you are a principal of a school, look at the academic calendar and syllabus. The portions to be covered, the number of lectures to be taken, etc. have to be planned. Also, involve the other teachers. After all, it is the teachers who will have to take those lectures.

While doing this, also take a look at the holidays, the exams to be held and the government policies. It helps to have a practical approach in planning.

Have a team

One can't work and complete tasks in isolation. There has to be a team that will work together towards the goal set. But the leader has to empower the team to go ahead and achieve the set goal.

The leader cannot just sit in his office and review the progress. It is important to have your feet on the ground. So being in touch with the team members and their real concerns is essential. You are where you are because of the team that backs you up. So support them when they need it. They may not always ask. But that's the point of a great leader. He knows exactly when he's needed.

Review daily

Take regular stock of the progress of the work. The daily basis review formula works even today.

The principal can take the daily attendance records, check what the teachers have taught the whole day, monitor the activities of the day, take a walk round the school or college campus for a surprise check. These are among the daily reviews that can happen.

And finally, at the end of the year, when the students

have been taught the full syllabus and they have passed their exams successfully, it's time to rejoice! Similarly, when your company achieves all the goals it set for itself, then the only thing left for you to do is to celebrate it.

Celebrate the success with everyone. It is due to the effort of one and all that the goals were achieved.

And remember, as a leader, give full credit to your team members for the success.

40

Happiness of Others

WHAT WAS CHANAKYA'S vision of an ideal leader?

A king who always thinks of the welfare of his people. That's his priority, come what may. And Chanakya believed that one must hone this kind of attitude in oneself. It is a leader with such an attitude that naturally draws the unwavering support of those around him.

Always remind yourself of what your end goal is—the happiness of others. This outlook will put you on the path to be a great leader one day. It does not matter if you are a leader of a thousand employees or just one person. It does not matter even if you do not have a single person reporting to you. If you work well and seek to fulfil the dreams of others as much as your own, you will eventually have a loyal following. So start preparing for the leadership role right now.

Let us see what secrets Chanakya reveals about what it takes to be a leader.

This is the most famous sutra from the *Arthashastra*, the

ultimate message on leadership. If one understands this sutra and imbibes it, the person is bound to become a towering personality.

Chanakya says,

'In the happiness of the subjects lies the benefit of the king and in what is beneficial to the subjects is his own benefit.' (1.19.34)

Consider this situation—a girl is about to be married. What do you think her father would be focused on, on the day of her wedding? He will obviously be completely focused on making sure that the marriage and all its arrangements are in place.

Now, during lunchtime does he think of eating himself?

No. He will want the guests to be fed properly. And in their happiness he will find his happiness.

Similarly, the leader has to think like a parent, and think of his subordinates and juniors as his children. This way, whatever he does will be for their benefit.

And what *can* one do to make sure their juniors and subordinates are happy?

How can you become a good leader at your workplace?

Make a list

It is important to know your subordinates and juniors. Some people just focus on the work at hand, and give little or no importance to the people who work under them. Make a list and study the requirements of each person. It can be one person working under you, or you could be leading a thousand people in an organization.

Understand their needs and what would actually make them happy or ease their burden in some way. Make a list of that also. For example, the salaries to be given on time, good infrastructure, support of systems, etc. If any of these things are missing, you must ensure it gets fixed right away.

Appreciate them

Appreciation is a human need. There are times when people, and the hard work they put in, go totally unnoticed. Therefore, it is important to build a system where each person's contribution is recognized by others. This is one of the healthiest practices to follow, one that the best companies across the globe incorporate in their offices.

Create a rewards-and-awards programme in your company. Introduce a 'best employee of the year' award. This will boost their morale. It will make them feel needed.

Even on a daily basis, make sure you appreciate your employees' good work. Give them a pat on the back. Take someone out for lunch. Give a small gift. These small gestures matter more than you know.

Think for them

Oftentimes employees themselves do not know what it is that they need. They may think that a secure and permanent job with a regular salary is enough. That is a myth.

You need to look beyond what they demand. Think about their future. Insurance, training and development, education, a sponsored trip—these are all concerns that will eventually cross any employee's mind. It's just a matter of when. So stay ahead by addressing such concerns in advance. This will only make you a more respected leader.

I have personally known owners of companies who even get involved in the planning of their employees' children's weddings. In that sense, they consider the children of their employees their own.

In this manner, the leader becomes a parent for everyone associated with the company.

For a good leader doesn't just build businesses, he builds families.

41

Once a Week

WEEKEND.

What comes to your mind when you read that word? Reprieve? Finally, a break from the toils of the week?

It's true that our lives revolve around the weekend. And why not? It's the only time we get to properly rejuvenate ourselves. To be productive at work and in life, it is important to compartmentalize our weeks that are dotted with these short, two-day breaks.

But it's important to plan this time of your week so you can make the most of it.

This time of the week must totally be for review and introspection of the work *done* and the work *to be done*.

So think about the day's activities, plan, make a roadmap, mark out corrections and gather information among others.

The best day to do this kind of a once-a-week review of one's activities could be a Saturday or a Sunday.

Why Saturday or Sunday? This is because there is less

distraction and workload on these days as compared to any other day of the week.

Why is this weekly time with yourself necessary?

Because Chanakya says,

> 'The affairs of a king are of three kinds—directly perceived, unperceived and inferred.' (1.9.4)

What is the main activity of a leader—it is to think!

If you want to be a leader at your workplace, you'll need to spend a considerable amount of time deliberating on what your team needs, the concerns that need to be addressed, etc.

So how is one supposed to think? Chanakya has given us relevant guidance in the verse above. He says a king will gather information from three sources. And based on these three sources he will then analyse the information and take critical decisions.

> 'What is seen by (the king) himself is directly perceived. What is communicated by others is unperceived. Forming an idea of what has not been done from what is done in respect of undertakings is inferred.' (1.9.5-7)

Here, Chanakya is again telling us in detail what he means by directly perceived, unperceived and inferred. Seen directly, reported by others and making an assumption—these are thus the three activities of the leader.

But with so much information floating around, it becomes difficult to even sit down, think and analyse. Therefore, once a week, it is important to take out time just to do this and nothing else.

So how do we start on this?

Fix a weekly time with yourself

Take out about one to two hours once in a week to just be with yourself and do an activity that requires you to use your mental faculties rigorously. Make sure you have no distractions during that time. Saturday or Sunday is suggested, but some are comfortable on a Friday evening, and some on Monday mornings.

Also, some are comfortable taking time out at work, while some would prefer to be at home. Some may even like to sit in a park and do it. Let it be at your comfort and convenience. This is the most important time with oneself.

List down

Try to have the data ready when you are doing this weekly exercise. Don't just think, put it on paper too. Do carry a notebook or a laptop for this activity. You can use your mobile phone too.

Make a list of things you are currently doing—your various tasks, role at work and in personal life, goals to be achieved. This list-preparation itself is a major task. But it's crucial because it offers clarity. Once you know everything you have on your plate, it'll be easier for you to tackle your problems one by one.

Look back and plan ahead

Once you take stock of all work you have ahead of you, it can be an eye-opening moment. A friend of mine who did this exercise said with wonder, 'I did not know that I am handling hundreds of minor and major projects.' So I'd like to let you know in advance that that list will be a revelation for sure.

Now segregate the things on that list, based on what needs to be started, what's in progress and what has already been completed or is near-completion.

Now look at your calendar and fix a day and time for these activities. For example, schedule an interview of a new candidate on Wednesday at 3 p.m. or a meeting with your sales team on Monday, 12 noon.

On a daily basis

So start your Monday mornings by looking at the list of things you planned do and stay focused on it. As you keep crossing things off that list, you will feel the satisfaction that you seek. Make a daily habit of reviewing your plan.

Thus, once you start diligently reviewing your tasks and doing things according to plan, you will be able to take up any new work sent your way and do so with confidence!

And remember, it is not about the amount of work you have in hand that should matter, but how you plan and handle it.

42

Appointing Managers

THERE ARE TWO stages in our careers—first, we get appointed; second, we appoint others.

In the beginning of our careers, we are judged by others. We have to join a company and work hard to prove ourselves. Later, when we become good at our jobs, we get a promotion. We start climbing up the corporate ladder.

The second stage of our career is drastically different from the first, because as opposed to earlier when you had to get things done yourself, now, you will have the power to get it done by others.

When a good salesman gets promoted, he ensures that the sales targets continue to be achieved by his team members. However, this is where most first-time managers usually fail.

A clear sign of growth in your career would be when the nature of your work changes over time. So as you grow and work towards your higher goal, even your work gets redefined. As the famous saying goes, 'If you continue doing what you are doing, you will continue getting what you are getting.' So stagnation is the enemy. You must keep evolving.

Therefore, Chanakya has given a roadmap for this. Start looking out for people who can join your team and get work done for you. Start planning the roles of your team members. Look out for your number two, someone who can replace you when you have moved up.

The skill to judge people and appoint the right person for the right job holds the key to your own growth.

In the *Arthashastra*, Chanakya even refers to other great teachers while appointing ministers for kings.

Here is a sutra,

'He should make his fellow-students his ministers, their integrity and capability being known to him,' says Bharadvaja. 'For, they enjoy his confidence.' (1.8.1)

There are various methods suggested in the *Arthashastra* as to how a king should appoint his ministers. One of the suggestions as given above is by Bharadvaja (associated with Drona, the celebrated teacher of the Kuru princes).

Just as the king had to appoint ministers, you too will one day have to appoint managers.

Bharadvaja suggested that one's classmates and childhood friends would be perfect candidates for managers. The reason is clear and simple. We've known them well over the years and therefore we can trust them. Their integrity and your confidence go hand in hand, after all.

But just being a friend is not enough. Here, Bharadvaja has pointed out that the candidate's capability is also an important yardstick. How much work s/he can handle is also an important question to ask before appointing someone.

So, here are practical tips to appoint your number two:

Look out on a daily basis

The truth is that you will never find your number two. You won't find your exact replacement. It is not like buying groceries across the counter in a store. We are dealing with human beings and every human being is different. The dynamics of each personality is different.

So on a daily basis, observe the people around you. Look out for that spark in the people around you. The way they handle their work; the way they communicate with others; their equation with the rest of the team; their behaviour and other qualities.

Interview them with others

You may find that a particular person is as good a manager as you are. But the fact is that you are only looking at it from your point of view. When the time finally comes to appoint the person, take a formal interview, regardless of how highly you think of them.

The golden rule, though, is never take the interview alone. Having multiple perspectives in such a case is of utmost importance. This is the reason why there's often a panel of experts at interviews.

Each person in the interview panel will be a value-addition from a different standpoint. For example, when IAS officers are interviewed, there are different people on the interview board, who ask different types of questions to gauge their competency on multiple levels. This helps diversify the quality of the set of questions in the interview.

Appoint, train and watch

Appointing a manager is not enough. This is only the beginning. There are several steps before the appointed manager becomes productive for you and the organization.

The next step is training them. The person might come from a totally different background. You will have to introduce him into the culture and working style of your organization. It takes time. So give the person his or her space. Train them, mentor them and give them the comfort that only comes with familiarity.

Give them a few months to settle down and after about six months you will find the person bloom into a really productive person.

Now he is ready to be your number two—your real manager.

43

Personal Income

SALARY AND INCOME are very important in our professional lives.

Even if we are working for free and have no expectations of being monetarily compensated, this should be discussed and made clear at the very beginning itself.

There are various reasons for which people join a profession.

Some join to gather experience in the initial stages of their career; some join for growth and higher income; some just wish to keep themselves busy. Some even continue to work post-retirement in order to pass on their experience and wisdom to others.

Whatever be the reason, the financial part has to be clear.

Chanakya always lends financial clarity before starting any work.

Even if you have a start-up business and do not have anything to pay yourself in the earlier stages, make sure your hard work is accounted for. I asked the founder of a start-up company about how he manages himself.

He said, 'I know my company cannot pay me at this stage. I have to pay my employees first. But I have made a provisional salary for myself. It is a figure put on my accounts. The day the company makes money, I will pick up the salary for all the months I have worked hard.' Now that is what financial clarity is all about.

He is working for money, but since there is no money in the company at the moment, he will pick it up later.

Another case:

A person has retired from a senior government position and has no financial liabilities. His children are settled in life. He has decent investments to take care of himself and his wife till death. He works now just to keep himself busy.

While joining a company's board of advisors, his financial deal was clear. 'I will not work for money, pay as per your budget for the work I do. But whenever I travel I keep a provision for me and my wife. Our travel expenses should be paid for by the company.'

Now he and his wife travel across the globe.

Thus, one needs to sort out the income at the very outset of one's work.

Chanakya has a clear idea about how much to pay his people:

'All undertakings are dependent on the treasury. Therefore, he should look into the treasury first.' (2.8.1)

Before you start any activity, do a financial calculation. This is a must. Chanakya makes it the number one priority.

There are some steps that one can follow to have clarity on financials and income:

Discuss finances openly

It is always a challenge to discuss money matters. But in professional life, remember, nothing is free. There are no free lunches. Therefore, discuss finances openly with your seniors.

Even if you want to give your services free of cost, let that be your choice. There are many social and spiritual organizations where there are people who work for free. But the same organizations have paid employees as well. Be clear which side you want to be associated with. This will help avoid a lot of confusion in the long run.

There is a non-government organization, where the CEO is working for a social cause. He is from a very rich family and loves his work. He just takes Re. 1 as his monthly salary. But he makes sure that all the expenses related to his work are taken care of by the organization.

Invest wisely

Saving and investment are key to financial success. One has to learn the art of investing wisely. Even if you are earning a salary, make sure you have a plan for saving and investment.

Invest in a diversified manner. Fixed deposits, mutual funds and other forms of savings will help you be financially free in the future.

The golden rule of investment is that you must be able to sustain yourself financially for minimum six months without an income. If yes, then you have taken the first step towards financial freedom in your life. Make sure you keep going on this path.

Let money work for you

In the earlier stages, you work for money. Later, let money work for you. This is the way to plan.

Your personal income should not be dependent on any organization. In fact, you should contribute to the income of your company.

There are two kinds of people in this world. First, who run behind money. Be the second kind, the ones who money is running after.

Let us all become the second kind.

44

Making Profits

IN ONE'S PROFESSIONAL life, financial profit is an important indicator of success.

Of course, making money by just about any method is not acceptable. The money has to be legally and ethically earned.

But it's also important to remind yourself that just being morally upright and honest is not enough. As a leader and good administrator, one has to make sure that one stays on the righteous path and at the same time brings in profits. This combination is what we should all aim for.

Chanakya had given similar advice in the *Arthashastra* when he said,

'The wise administrator should fix the revenue and show and increase in income and decrease in expenditure and should remedy the opposite of these.' (2.6.28)

An administrator of a company is the one who runs the show on a daily basis. To ensure financial profitability is one of his key responsibilities.

So, Chanakya says, the administrator should first fix the revenue. Meaning, he should fix a target for his division. This will give him an exact goal, a purpose to go ahead and achieve. We have seen in the previous chapters how a leader sets a yearly target and reviews it regularly to achieve it. This is no different.

Next, the administrator should show an increase in income. Meaning, he should try and exceed the expectations of his superiors. So he needs to try to achieve more than the target he set for himself. Not just that, the target he sets should always exceed previous targets.

Decreasing revenue is completely counter-productive. That is not success at all. In fact, it's the opposite of success, regardless of how high this revenue is. One should be able to show growth on a consistent basis. You can't outshine one year and then dip in the other.

Next is to decrease expenditure. This is quintessential to any good business. The cost of running a company has to be cut down from time to time. Take a look at your balance sheet and check the areas that draw maximum expenditure. Try to identify parts of it that could absorb cost reduction and implement the same.

So carrying out both the tasks hand in hand—increase in income and reduction in expenditure—are the two key aspects any good manager has to focus on.

If the reverse of this happens, then it will inevitably lead to failure. Decrease in income and increase in expenditure is a sure path to disaster.

Here's what you can do to get the balance right:

Check the balance sheet

Balance sheet is a great indicator of an organization's financial health. These are audited statements and contain the macro and micro picture of how the organization is doing. It is usually prepared by professionals like chartered accountants.

If you are a beginner at reading balance sheets, then it is advisable that you seek professional help. There is a lot to learn if one is to understand the financial intricacies of a company. The essence of a balance sheet is PAT i.e. Net Profit After Taxes. This is the bottom line.

Work on income

Look at the revenue sources of the organization. Depending on the type of organization, revenues could come from multiple sources. If it is a government organization, the revenue could come from taxes or it could even be self-generating income sources. Most private companies are dependent on their customers and clients for income sources. Educational and charitable organizations get their revenues from donations and grants.

So prepare a plan to increase the sources of income. Make sure there are more clients to your list of existing customers. If you have ten customers, make sure you add more customers and make it fifteen, or twenty. That should be your immediate goal. Or offer new products and services to your clients. Diversify into new markets. New ideas always help. Keep looking for new opportunities.

Work on reduction

The next aspect to studying the balance sheet of your company is to study how much is being spent under each department. There you will gain a similar insight. Some expenses are necessary, while some are not. For example, in government even though defence and security, like police , are never revenue sources, they are quintessential for the safety and security of the people. So those are things that can't be compromised on in any manner.

However, there are many things that are necessary but can be outsourced. For example, the housekeeping person doesn't have to be on the payroll or be a permanent employee of the company. That cost can be reduced in a substantial way. Have a contract with a facility-management company, and they will ensure a good price as well as the same quality of service you're used to.

When you practise these things, you're bound to see the net profit grow.

If you successfully pull this off, then as an administrator you are already in high demand in the job market.

45

Board of Experts

YOU ARE A reflection of the people you choose to surround yourself with.

Therefore, it is essential that you choose these people carefully, that they form a team of experts who can give you the right guidance every step of the way.

There are many methods through which you can surround yourself with experts. One would be to approach them, and then invite them to be part of your board of advisors or experts. Even the government has made it mandatory to have independent directors on the board of companies.

Chanakya had many such organizational designs made, through which the leader can get expert advice on how a company functions.

The king had a council of ministers to advise him. The raj guru and chaplin were among the different mentors Chanakya suggested the king should have as advisors. Through them he would build his plans and strategies.

All the kings back in the day had such a board of experts to advise them. Akbar had a panel called the navratnas (nine gems) who were experts from various fields. Chatrapati Shivaji of Maharashtra had eight experts on his team called ashta-pradhan.

Many large organizations, in the government and private sectors, have committees that play this role.

In the chapter Appointment of Councillors (book 1, chapter 9) of the *Arthashastra*, Chanakya gives a symbolic interpretation of how a king becomes successful because of a board of experts guiding him.

Chanakya says,

'Kshatriya power, made to prosper by the Brahmin (chaplain), sanctified by spells in the form of the council of ministers, (and) possessed of arms in the form of compliance with the science (of politics), triumphs, remaining ever unconquered.' (1.9.11)

This is a powerful statement made on the basis of Indian culture. The Hindu tradition has a system of rituals which Chanakya is using as an analogy here to make his point. Kshatriya is the ruler class. The leaders are made to prosper by the Brahmins, as it is the Brahmins who are the teachers.

The king was made successful by his teacher. The raja and the guru combination is a model that has been followed since ancient India—Chanakya and Chandragupta, Shivaji and Ramdas, among others.

The next set of experts was the council of ministers. The king was advised by them on matters of national importance.

Akbar and Birbal, Krishnadevaraya and Tenalirama—these are famous examples as well. The experts would always give strategic inputs on any matter related to security, etc. And they did this in compliance with the science of politics (as given in the scriptures). The kings of ancient India would refer to the *Dharmashastra* and the *Arthashastra* to make sure that they were on the right path.

Thus, the combination of inputs from these three sources—gurus, ministers and scriptures—ensured that the king was successful forever, which is another way of saying that he remained unconquered.

Let us follow these steps to appoint our very own board of experts:

Find the experts

One may feel that experts are not available. Or that their consultation fees might be very high. This couldn't be far from the truth. But they are always available and most of them would be happy to provide their expertise at a nominal rate or even free of charge.

Take the initiative to reach out to people. They could be retirees from a large organization and now sitting idle at home. They could be found in various universities. Professors are after all experts of their own fields and have a lot of knowledge and wisdom.

Drink the nectar of wisdom from these experts. Just make a wish and they will come to you. They are ready to give, and you should be ready to accept.

Offer a formal position

It is not enough to know them and approach them. Offer them a formal position in your company. Like the kings of ancient India gave them some status in their court, you should also offer them a good position in your board of experts. Formally invite them to your board meetings and ask for their inputs.

Even though most of them will not expect money, do pay them whatever you can. Treat the money given to them as guru dakshina.

Respect and honour is what these experts require from you. They will take care of the rest. And to add to it, they will also bring their contacts to help you.

Beyond board meetings

Now, do not make it so formal that you lose your personal touch with these experts. Develop your relationship with them, like a guru and a shishya. Be childlike in front of them. Be ready to learn from them at every step.

Serve them, look after them and take care of them. Do that on a daily basis.

It is said in our culture that those who serve and listen to their elders will never face any problems in life.

This type of attitude is called vriddha-sanyogah, which means being in constant touch with your elders.

It's a time-tested and sure route to eternal success.

46

Retirement Plan

WHICH IS THE day you begin to plan for your retirement?

Is it on the last day of your office? No.

The day you join the office is when you should start planning for your last day there.

When a person is born, there is one thing that is certain—death.

Similarly, our professional lives will also end one day. Nothing is permanent, including our jobs. Everything will one day come to a halt.

But most people don't plan their retirement in a proactive manner, especially during the early stages of their careers. Everyone just goes with the flow, till one day it hits them that their work lives are over.

Many find it hard to handle. Working becomes a habit that they can't shake off. So a sudden break brings their lives to a halt.

It's worse for a government employee at a senior post.

Because s/he has been working continuously for almost thirty to forty years. Then one day s/he loses his or her power, identity and self-esteem. S/he does not know what to do next.

And the planning is essential not only at a personal level, but also on the part of the organization. If the person leaves and there is no appropriate replacement for him or her, then the work is bound to suffer in a major way.

So what is the solution?

Chanakya has a unique way of looking at things. The solution for having a legacy is to train people from the younger generation. Those who can be leaders in the long run.

He says,

> **'He (king) should strive to give training to the prince.'**
> **(5.6.39)**

The king should be able to see long term. As we had seen earlier, after Grihasta-ashram (an active life) every person, according to the Vedic Indian culture, has to plan for Vana-prastha (a retired life). And their plan should be one that makes it a smooth transition.

So, two things have to be done during the working phase of your life. First, get ready to retire as soon as possible. Second, train the next generation to take your place and position.

So here are some tips to plan your exit strategy from your career.

Think of death

On a daily basis, think of death for a few minutes. Now, this may seem strange, and sometimes frightening too. But this will give you a different perspective on life itself. It will be difficult in the beginning but it will give you the confidence to accept death as part of life.

So, when you look at your own desk every day, think for a few minutes on these lines—what if I am not there; will the work still go on? Who will do the work when I am not around? Can I be replaced by someone better than me?

Train others

Your experience should not go to waste at all. And the answer to the questions asked above will make you strive to train the young people in your organization. Create more leaders. A real leader is one who creates leaders.

Also, learn to trust your juniors to work and do better than yourself. Many people are not comfortable with the idea of imparting all their knowledge to their subordinates, because they feel like they are creating competitors for themselves.

Also, this question is generally asked—what if I train them and they leave the company? The answer to the question is another strange question—what if you don't train them and they stay? So it's better if you train them.

Be happy about your retirement

Someone asked a spiritual master, 'If death comes to you, what would you say?' He said in excitement, 'I would tell him, why are you so late? I have been waiting for such a long time to meet you. Come on. Let's go.'

In the same way, you should look forward to your last day at work.

It should not be the saddest day of your life. On the contrary, it should be the happiest day of your life. After all, you have done your best and you're now leaving a legacy behind.

And most importantly, you still have lots of time and energy left to do the best thing—spend quality time with your family and friends.

Go ahead and retire with grace.

The next chapter of your life is just waiting to start.

FAMILY LIFE

47

Duties of a Householder

SO FAR, WE have learned how to apply Chanakya's wisdom in our personal and professional lives, in Part One and Part Two, respectively.

Now we come to the third part—applying Chanakya's wisdom in family life.

Our lives are incomplete without our families. Especially in India, where the culture itself promotes a strong bond within the family, placing the highest importance to sticking to one's roots. Our joint family system, our large extended family of grandparents, uncles and aunts, cousins are all a crucial part of our society.

So, success in personal and professional life does not automatically translate to being a successful person. To be called a 'totally' successful person also requires one to be a successful family person, the third and most important dimension.

So, let us begin this section with a look at the duties of a householder.

The duties of a householder, or Grihastha, have already been defined in the Vedas. The Vedas are the oldest books available to mankind. Our culture is defined by these texts to a great degree.

Chanakya also takes his inspiration of setting up an ideal kingdom and society based on the Vedic system in the *Arthashastra*.

He says,

'The duties of a householder are: earning his living in accordance with his own special duty; marrying into the families of the same caste, but not of the same gotra; approaching the wife during the (right) time; worship of gods, Manes and guests; making gifts to dependents and eating what is left over (after the others have eaten).'
(1.3.9)

We will be looking at each of these aspects/duties of a family person over the next few chapters. Note that the duties are relevant to both women and men. It is important to understand that a family will not be complete without the compatibility of both the husband and the wife. So finally it is the mutual respect between them that will make for a successful family.

Let us look into the first aspect:

'Duties of a householder are: earning in accordance with his own special duty.' (1.3.9)

The first and foremost duty of a householder is to earn a living for his family.

This is a very practical advice given by Chanakya. Earning

the bread and butter for one's family members is essential. The children, the elders and, in a larger sense, the society depends on the earning members.

'Dhanyo Grihasta-ashram,' say our Indian scriptures. It means 'great and blessed is the life of a householder'. It is due to them that the society can sustain, maintain and prosper.

But how must a householder earn in accordance with his own special duty? The word used in Sanskrit is swa-dharma. Swa—self, dharma—natural. So, one should earn through a means which is natural to a person.

Let us understand this better:

Our natural talent

Each person is blessed with a unique talent. Once you find what your unique quality is, your whole life will change. This talent will come naturally to you. It might be your natural tendency to be an artist or a sportsperson or even a businessperson. Earn your living through that. Don't follow other people's footsteps. Pave your own way.

Our problem is that we try and earn a living without much thought about the means by which we're doing so. So, at the end of the journey, even if we have made money, we find ourselves devoid of happiness. So find what makes you happy.

Our education system

It is unfortunate that our current education system does not allow us to explore our natural talent. We did not create an education system; instead, we have created an examination system.

Our ancient education system was designed to first explore your talents and find what you are good at. And then slowly train you and help you make a career out of it. This kind of system also made a person feel worthy. Try to find a way to revisit that old model.

Find your swa-dharma

So, how do you find your swa-dharma? Observe yourself on a daily basis. What makes you happy? There must be some activity which does not frustrate you at all. When you do that, you feel like time is flying away.

It could be related to the arts, science or even sports. Once you know, go after this passion, and try and make a career out of it.

So along with earning money for your family, you will find true happiness even in your profession.

48

Marriage—a Choice

MARRIAGE IS A very important aspect of one's family life.

What is a marriage? It's a question that requires more introspection than one might presume. Most of us consider it a social relationship which has to be fulfilled. And when we get into wedlock without clarity, we get frustrated for life.

Understand that marriage is not just a social obligation, but a divine duty to be fulfilled. Know this fully well before you get married. Marrying out of pressure will only take you away from the path to lifelong happiness. Sometimes, it is better not to marry and be happy, than to get married and feel frustrated throughout life.

There are happily unmarried people too in this world, just as there are happily married people. Remember, the key word is 'happy'. Happiness is what you should seek in your life, married or not.

But if you do decide to get married, then the next step is to find a suitable spouse.

There is a saying that goes, 'The marriage partner you choose will define your life in a significant way. Your lifelong happiness would depend on that one decision.'

There are many traditional systems in India to find a compatible life partner.

Chanakya mentions one such method as the duty of a householder,

'The duties of a householder are: marrying into families of the same caste, but not of the same gotra.' (1.3.9)

The ancient caste system of India was its strength. But unfortunately, in our generation it has become one of its weaknesses.

Think of a caste as a community of like-minded people. They have the same traditional practices, rituals, food habits, social events, etc. Now, when you get married to a person from a similar community, then it is very easy to adjust for both parties involved.

There are many instances where even love marriages have failed. Oftentimes the reason for this has been that after getting married, both partners realized that they could not adjust themselves to the families of their spouse.

I am not against love marriage, but I like to take these differences into consideration to have a holistic view of this institution. Take everything into account, so that you can anticipate the changes you'll need to adjust to, in order to become an ideal couple.

So how should you choose your partner in a traditional and non-traditional manner? Here's how:

Arranged marriage

Be it arranged or love marriage, Chanakya has said that one should not get married into one's own gotra, in other words, the family lineage. So basically the children of two brothers should not get married to each other. Or children from sibling sisters should not marry each other. It has been medically proven that children born from such marriages face various mental disorders.

Marriages among cousins is an accepted norm in various communities across India. But remember, the partners have to be from a different gotra, another bloodline.

Another traditional practice to find the compatibility among would-be life partners is to match their horoscopes. This unique method also helps determine the 'psychological' compatibility.

Arranged love marriage

Every generation has its own timeless tales of successful love marriages.

If two people are in love with each other, they should get married.

But what about the parents? That too in a society where going against the wishes of one's parents is considered a deadly sin? Simple answer is, get them involved in your marriage. Let them 'arrange' your love marriage.

It may take some time to convince them, but have patience. It'll be worth it. Let the parents of both partners meet and understand each other. Let them arrive at the beauty of your union on their own. Then the journey will be smooth.

It still requires effort

Marriage may be made in heaven but we need to make it work on earth. Be it arranged or love marriage, there is a lot of effort to be put into it. It is a continuous process of discovering each other, even as you discover yourself. Learn to respect the differences and different views of your partner. It only enriches your bond.

A wise man was asked, 'Sir, what do you suggest, a love marriage or an arranged marriage?' With a smile he said, 'I suggest a successful marriage.'

49

Sex in Marriage

SEX IS A very important part of married life.

Until recently, discussing sex was considered a taboo in our society.

Due to the vast and freely available information on the Internet and media, people are far more open to discussing this topic.

In fact, to a large extent, it is still considered degrading and immoral to discuss this openly, but many are warming up to the idea.

But it's time to face the reality. Many marriages end because of the issues that take place inside the bedroom. Instead of hiding the facts, let us discuss this in a mature manner and find solutions.

Have you heard about the concept of 'marital rape'? It is quite shocking, but it is a very real part of married life that is now getting exposed in a big way. Rape is the most brutal form of violation; it leaves a lifelong scar on the mind of the victim. Now, imagine, what if this is done by one's own husband on a daily basis?

Many women are now taking this matter to court. But the solution is not just legal. It has to do with providing sex education to married couples. It's better to start before they get married. The first thing needed in a marriage, if one is to find happiness at a physical level, is mutual respect.

Therefore, Chanakya says,

> **'The duties of a householder are: approaching the wife during the (right) time.' (1.3.9)**

The best part of Chanakya's teachings is that he has openly discussed every topic under the sun. He educates both the husband and the wife about the physical aspect of married life.

There are many scholarly references that the *Kamasutra* of Vatsyayana was also written by Chanakya under a different name. There, he gives details about the best way two partners can have sex, based on mutual respect.

It is suggested that one read the original Sanskrit version of the *Kamasutra* with a scholarly approach. Sadly, the current perception about the *Kamasutra* is that it is just about various physical postures during sex. That is just one part of it.

The *Kamasutra* insists on mental compatibility over physical compatibility. Hygiene, timing and the stress on celebrating each other gives it an aspect of divinity. That is why it is respected across the globe in the intellectual community. It is one of India's unique contributions to world literature when it comes to a relationship between two people.

So, as we see in the above sutra, Chanakya says it is the

duty of the householder to approach his wife at the right time.

Let us understand this a little better:

Right time

Human beings are different from animals because there is an important aspect of morality connected to sex. Animals have sex as an impulse. They do not think too much about it. But nature has its own method to control them, as they have mating seasons.

But for human beings there is no particular mating season or time. So one has to decide what the right time and place is. Sex is a private matter between two partners, so only when they both are ready should they come together. But when the woman goes through her monthly period, it is to be avoided for medical and hygiene reasons. Right time also refers to the time when the body is most fertile.

Children

Remember, the objective of sex in marriage is not just pleasure alone. It is to have children too. Marriage is about taking one's family lineage forward.

There are many methods in our Indian scriptures which show that you can actually have the kind of children you want. By planning correctly in advance, children can be a choice, not an accident. The right soul can be invited to come into the mother's womb. Children born from such foresighted couples prove to be child prodigies, extremely brilliant and spiritual in nature.

Discuss openly

The most important way to have a healthy sex life is to discuss it openly. There should be no barriers between a husband and wife. Express your feelings to your partner. If you are not mentally and physically ready for sex, tell them. Your partner should respect your boundaries.

On the other hand, when you want to have it, express that too. After all, it is not just a physical need, but an emotional one too. Your honesty and mutual respect will only bring you closer together.

50

House Becomes a Temple

A WOMAN MAKES a house a home.

A family makes a house a temple.

A temple, church, mosque or a gurudwara—they're all places of worship, places where you remember God. When you enter such a place of worship, your mind becomes calm and quiet.

A householder is called a Grihasta-ashram in Sanskrit. 'Grih' is home, and 'ashram' is a spiritual place. Therefore, in the Hindu tradition, the home is equated to a spiritual retreat.

What is your first emotion when you think about your home? Do you feel tense or is it a place you look forward to going to?

If the very thought of home comforts you, then you've managed to capture the essence of the term Grihasta-ashram. If not, then Chanakya has some priceless advice on the matter.

He says,

'The duties of a householder are: worship of gods, Manes and guests.' (1.3.9)

There is a traditional house-warming ceremony in India called Grihapravesh, which is performed on the first day of moving into the house. This involves a pooja performed by a pandit and helps cleanse the house.

The pandit establishes a place of worship in a small space inside the house and this is where a temple is then set up. This is where every family member prays on a daily basis. Not many are aware that the first god to be worshipped in a house is the fire god, 'Agni'.

The Rig Veda, the first among the four Vedas and the earliest document of human history, starts with worshipping the fire god. This rule is followed till date. During the house-warming ceremony, fire is worshipped through the yagna ritual. From then onwards, residents of the house are expected to light a lamp in front of the home temple every day.

And, as suggested by Chanakya in the above sutra, it is one's duty to worship the gods, Manes and guests on a daily basis.

How should we remember them every day?

Your faith

In God we trust. It is our unwavering faith in God that helps us sail through the challenges of life effortlessly. Therefore, worshipping God is a healthy practice. We might do so just at the beginning of our day, but the truth is that that feeling of divinity stays with us throughout the day.

Each person in the family may have his or her personal

deity of liking. It does not matter what form of God it is. But you must begin each day with worshipping them.

Your family

Next is the worship of the Manes. They are our ancestors, our forefathers. We are a reflection of our past. We are because they were. One cannot take all credit for what one does. A quick look at any family will show you that it has its own unique tradition or 'parampara'.

I may remember my father, my grandfather and maybe a couple of generations before that. But is it possible to remember our families beyond that?

Our rishis were so intelligent that they made something called the gotra system. It allows every person to trace his ancestry. These days it's quite popular to look for one's lineage or family tree. Many call it 'finding your roots'. But our tradition has an inbuilt system that doesn't let us forget them.

Your guests

Last but not the least, worship your guests. In Sanskrit, a guest is called atithi. 'Tithi' means date and time, 'a' means without.

Our tradition thus gives the guest complete freedom to come to our house at any given point of time.

The famous mantra from *Taittiriya Upanishad* says, 'Atithi Devo Bhava', meaning, consider your guests as gods. The Government of India also used this mantra for its tourism promotion campaign during the branding activity of 'Incredible India' across the globe.

When you follow all these three practices on a daily basis,

your house will become a blessed place. It will have a different vibration altogether. One will not only feel safe and secure here, but also wanted and important.

May each house become such an ashram.

Let our ancestors be proud of us.

Let them feel happy that we have not only kept the tradition alive, but taken it forward with pride and a feeling of gratitude.

51

Taking Care of Family Members

YOUR FAMILY COMPLETES you. No matter what you achieve in life and how far you travel, it is your family that you will always find comfort in, that you'll always want to return to.

Lucky are those who have a family and are brought up with love and care. Having parents, siblings, relatives is indeed a great blessing. There are so many orphans in the world who do not enjoy such a fortune.

Of course, every family has its own set of differences and share of fights. But that's the thing about a family—it stays together. That is its biggest strength. And families are ecosystems that help us stay grounded. You may be the most successful person in the world, but you will still be a son or daughter to your parents. You will still have show them the same respect as was always expected of you.

And the love your family showers you with is unconditional. Be it success or failure, families are great equalizers.

Therefore, it is the responsibility of each family member

to take care of the others.

The love and concern for family members is expressed by Chanakya in the following sutra:

'The duties of a householder are: making gifts to dependents and eating what is left over (after the others have eaten).' (1.3.9)

Chanakya says that in a family there could be earning members and non-earning members. Those earning should take care of the rest.

Usually the dependents are the elders, whose working life is over, or children, who have not yet started earning. There could also be those who have some physical disability or other problems.

By gifts Chanakya simply means, give them enough to take care of themselves.

And you should be happy to take care of your dependents, instead of treating it like a burden.

Another point Chanakya makes is about food habits. Eat only after feeding others and only that which is left over. Prioritize your family.

Usually it is said that the women of the house should follow the three Ls with regards to eating—last, least and leftover.

But Chanakya advises every householder, including the male members, to follow these habits.

Let us look at how we should practise them in our daily lives:

When you reach home

Whenever you reach home after a long day of work, just spend some time with your family. Even if you are tired. These moments you spend with your children, your spouse and your elders will be moments that will be cherished by all of you for as long as you live.

Share your finances

If you are the earning member of the family, make sure you share your money with others. Remember, you never earn for yourself, you earn for your family. Give some pocket money to your children, siblings and aged people. And always give a little more than what they need. They will forever be grateful.

An important tip for the husband whose wife is not an earning member—do not think that just because she stays at home to take care of the kids instead of going out to work like you, she is not doing anything. That's far from the truth. In fact, her job is probably harder than yours to begin with. She takes care of the family, looks after the children and feeds you all. That is a worthy contribution. So give her money too. And give enough that she does not have to think twice before spending on herself.

Food at home

You are lucky if you get to eat food every day. Every meal you have is something to be grateful for. There are millions of people across the globe who do not get two square meals a day. If your refrigerator is full and you do not have to worry about your next meal, thank God for that privilege.

So when you come home, make sure everyone, including the servants, has had their food. Only then feed yourself.

Regardless of whether you are rich or poor, you must share whatever food you have with others around you.

A poor hard-working man once told his wife, 'One day we will be rich.' The wife looked into his eyes and said, 'We are already rich, we have each other. One day we will have money too.'

If you are loved by friends and family, then as far as I'm concerned, you're the richest person alive.

52

Educating Children

IT IS SAID that when Chanakya was looking for an ideal disciple to replace the unjust king Dhana Nanda, he found Chandragupta Maurya in a village.

Chandragupta came from a poor background and hadn't received any education. Chanakya identified the leadership qualities in him and wanted to educate and train him further. So, he went to Chandragupta's mother and asked for her permission to send him for higher education.

Chandragupta's mother, a poor woman herself, did not know what to do and so she asked her brother. The uncle in turn saw a financial opportunity and asked Chanakya to pay a high sum to take away the young boy. In reality he was selling the boy.

With no other option in sight, Chanakya paid him and took Chandragupta away for higher education. Later, he groomed him to become the king and samrat of Bharat. It is said that after defeating Dhana Nanda, when Chandragupta was crowed the king, the first decision Chanakya took was to call the mother and uncle.

The order was given to put the uncle to death. This was a shocking decision for everyone, including the grown-up Chandragupta. When asked why, Chanakya said,

'For me, the greatest crime is a child denied the opportunity to study. Let this be an example set for others, that no one should ever do that.'

Therefore, the prime duty of a family person is to make sure that his children get the education they so deserve.

Chanakya says,

'The wise person should groom their children carefully to make them persons of high qualities and see them employed in productive work. Only the persons of learning and qualities find respect in the society.'
(Chanakya Niti [CN], 2.10)

This story from the life of Chanakya, along with the verse from *Chanakya Niti*, sends one important message to all family members—educate your children without compromise.

And consider what kind of grooming and upbringing they should get carefully. Care is feeling that children understand easily. So with love and concern, bring up your kids.

The parents who educate their children are called wise. What happens when you educate your children? They become persons of high quality. Educated persons are respected in the world. If you compare an educated person and a wealthy person, the highly educated person is more respected. The best is to be a wealthy person who is highly educated. Strive to become a parent who inculcates these qualities in his children.

Education and degrees alone are not enough. Make sure your children earn a living. So, employ them in productive work. That does not mean just give them a job and make them employed. It means they should have a purposeful living. Such children with high values and moral character will only find respect in society.

What are the steps you should take to educate your children?

Find the right school and teacher

Education is the very foundation of life. But you should carefully choose the right school along with the right teacher for your children.

Just pause a bit and think. They don't need to go to the most expensive school. Today, it has become a status symbol for parents to go for international boards without much thought. If you can afford it, go ahead. But unfortunately, many of these institutions have turned education into a business. So it goes without saying that you should choose the school based on its attention to the quality of education as well as competency of its teaching staff.

You monitor daily

Many think that once they've admitted their child to a good school and paid the fees, their job's done. The duty of parents does not end here. In fact, it has only just begun. The three important pillars that will help the child develop its character are parents, the school and the peer group.

And you as a parent must have an eye on all these three aspects. You must make sure they're not being deprived on any front. Without this, your parenting will be incomplete. Usually mothers are expected to be more hands-on with their children but fathers should feel equally responsible to do the same.

Remember, your child will not always be able to identify what's lacking, let alone articulate it. So you must at all times be sensitive to their educational, physical as well as emotional needs.

53

Family Prayer

A FAMILY THAT prays together, stays together.

This phrase exists in every culture across the world in some way or the other. It's true that if we make this a daily practice, it will strengthen the bond that exists among the members of our family.

Unfortunately, evenings are no longer family time at home. They have become TV time. With modern technology entering personal space, everyone is busy using their gadgets.

Now, technology is not bad at all. After all, it has allowed us to connect to friends and family members across the globe. There is hardly any cost involved too.

But remember, it has another side to it. Either you can use it or it can use you. Therefore, some self-regulation is essential.

So what is the solution to all this? Should we not watch TV or surf the Internet during evening hours? No, that is not what is to be done. After all, technology is an integral part of our lives.

The solution to the problem is totally different.

The way to connect with family members is through a common prayer time.

Chanakya suggests having a study and prayer time. This can be practised as an individual as well as with one's family.

'A man must read and study a shloka (Sanskrit couplet) every day. If it is not possible, read half of it, or a part of it or at least a word. Never let any day go without some study of a written word. One should make one's day fruitful by doing good work and study.' (CN 2.13)

Every person in the family should study the scriptures on a daily basis. A simple suggestion Chanakya gives is to at least study a shloka every day. There are many scriptures like the Ramayana, Bhagwad Gita, Srimad Bhagavatam or other regional or religious books.

Study one verse a day. Simple enough? And make it a habit.

Chanakya was also very perceptive. He could foresee how, eventually, the future generations might face time constraints. Hence, he includes time management in this study-and-prayer time. Studying one shloka hardly takes a few minutes. If you cannot do that or struggle to understand it completely, then read at least half of the shloka. If not that, then a small part of it. Or even just a word of it. But do that.

Come what may, make an effort to study a little each day. Not a single day should pass without studying the scriptures. Make each day a fruitful one.

So how does one practise this at the family level on a regular basis?

Start with yourself

What you want others to follow, you must first practise yourself. Take up reading any scripture you like. Every evening, sit near the place of worship in your house and pray for a few minutes. Following this, read a few pages of the scripture of your choice. If not, at least read one shloka, as suggested by Chanakya. Then try to understand its meaning and deeper significance. Think and reflect over it. Do this regularly and after a while you will feel an inner change come about.

Involve the family members

When you pray like this for the first time, other family members will be watching you. They may find it surprising, because they've never seen this side of your personality before.

Now, slowly involve them in your prayer and studies. Do not force anyone. Let them join you of their own accord. But be consistent in your practice. After some time, someone is bound to join you in your noble spiritual quest.

Make it a habit

When a few family members start do it consistently, it sends a strong message to the remaining ones. Even those who do not feel like doing it will eventually join you.

Such a habit or ritual is healthy for your family. This time spent together will put you on a spiritual journey with your loved ones. And only good can come of this.

54

Family Friends

WE ALL HAVE friends. Friends we make in school, in college, at work. And then there are the family friends.

Family friends hold a special place in our lives, as it's the coming together of two families.

Say you have an office colleague who is now your personal friend. One day you decide to invite him home for dinner. He may get his family along. Soon his wife and your wife become friends. Your children play together and become friends too.

This is very common and there have been many instances where such family friendships bloom into relationships in future. Even marriages may take place between the members of such family friends.

Chanakya appreciated this but also gave us a strict warning about what kind of family friends one should have. He said,

'One who befriends a person of bad character, a person of bad intentions, a person who is a sinner or a person who

lives at an evil place; gets destroyed in quick time.'
(CN 2.19)

His warning? Keep a distance.

Think hard before you befriend anyone. One should be friendly with everyone, but choosing close friends should be done with caution.

What kind of friends should be avoided? Those with bad character. These are the people who indulge in vices and immoral activities. Next on the list to be avoided are those with bad intentions—the people who will befriend you for personal gain. One may realize this all too late, when heavy loss is already upon them.

Trust. Don't over-trust. Avoid sinners and those who live in places that are infamous for criminal activity.

Why? Because bad company is enough to destroy everything you have built.

So you have to be extremely careful about the kind of people you bring home.

Think along these lines when allowing someone into your family:

Start with yourself

Take stock of your own friends. They could be schoolfriends or work friends. Some friends are made during a journey or some social interaction. With each person, take your time and understand their backgrounds.

The idea is not to be paranoid and assume that every person is bad. But take precautions before your friendship grows deeper. The more one spends time with a new person, the more you understand him or her better.

So observe the person's behaviour, the way they talk to/treat others, etc. People give away more than they think through their actions.

When you see goodness in someone, work hard at nurturing your friendship with them. Similarly, if you find that someone might pose a threat, slowly exit that relationship.

Look out for others

Keep an eye out on behalf of your family as well. Some members in the family, like children, aren't a good judge of character. We should be their guiding force. But this has to be handled in a subtle manner.

If you have a teenage daughter or son and you realize that they are in bad company, what do you do? You can't shout at them; it'll only drive them away from you. You will have to patiently make them realize the evil intentions of those people. Slowly and steadily, you'll have to make sure they get away from such dangerous friendships.

Good company is good

While you must distance yourself from bad company, you must also spend time developing good friends.

'Ku-sangh' is bad company, 'sat-sangh' is good. Adi Shankaracharya, the great Indian philosopher, placed a lot of importance on sat-sangh. He said that such noble company takes a person higher and higher in thoughts as well as actions, finally helping him attain moksha or self-realization.

Human beings require company. We're naturally social beings. We're not meant to be on our own. Besides, being a loner could lead to psychological and social problems.

So keep the company of the good, avoid the evildoers and be ready to develop new friendships.

Even when it comes to running a kingdom, Chanakya says that the king needs a good set of mitras (friends) to help him follow through, for it these mitras that will be by his side through good and bad times.

And remember, good times show you who your friends are. Bad times reveal who your *true* friends are.

55

Single Child

TIMES ARE CHANGING and so are parents and their parenting style.

From joint families, we are now turning into nuclear families. And many couples are now deciding to have just one child.

What is the reason for this? Well, financial constraints, time constraints, unaffordable housing, etc. All these practical reasons are now pushing new parents to limit themselves to being a family of three.

And though technology has made it rather easy for parents to keep in touch with their children, no matter which corner of the world they're in, it's still hard to be the parents of a single child. Because all your hopes and dreams are centred on this one child, and hence you expect a lot more.

What is Chanakya's take on parenting one child?

He said,

'If the only son comes as a scholar-gentleman, the family is lit up with joy, just like rising of the single moon spreads light into darkness.' (CN 3.16)

It does not matter if you have ten children or just one child. Parenting is not about numbers, it is about helping your child reach its full potential.

And this applies not only to a son, but is just as relevant to a daughter, despite what Chanakya mentions. Today there is no difference between a son and a daughter. Both are equal. In fact, in many cases daughters are preferred over boys. For instance, some communities in India, like the Nair community in Kerala, follow a matriarchal system, where the lady is the head of the family. So girls are given preference over boys.

So, let us look at what measures parents who have a single child need to take to raise their child in the best possible manner:

Do not differentiate

You could have a single child out of choice or because of compulsion. Choice, because you want to give the best to one child. Compulsion, because of financial constraints. Sometimes, people are unable to have a second child for biological reasons.

The first thing you need to do is accept the child as a gift from God. And never discriminate based on their gender. Do not compare them with other children on beauty, colour or even intelligence. Nothing is worth comparing your kid to another. You must accept him or her as they are.

Values

What makes a man a gentleman? His values. The way someone treats others says a lot about their character.

So, as a parent, it is important to bring up your child with such values. Instil kindness in them by being kind towards them. Teach them the value of things. Do not just buy them something. Teach them how to earn it. One of the risks of being a single child is that it's easy to feel pampered and lose perspective of the value of things. That's because the parents only have that one child and want to fulfil all its needs. So as a parent to a single child, you must also earn to exercise self-discipline, so as not to get carried away with pampering your child.

Social life

A single child is bound to miss out on the special and constant bond of siblings. And being by themselves might also lead them to become loners of sorts. So it is crucial that the family creates an interactive atmosphere where s/he does not feel hesitant to approach his or her parents, and doesn't for a moment feel the lack of company.

The social life of a single child definitely needs some attention and careful planning. Parents, grandparents, uncles and aunts are important for such a child. You also need to make sure that they spend a lot of time with other children in their school, cousins in the family and friends staying around.

Remember, no matter how your child turns out, you need to do your part. Let them know how much you love them and that you're proud of them each day. Do this and they will find no reason to let you down.

56

Secret of Good Parenting

PARENTING IS AN art and a science, because it involves the psychological training of a child.

That's what parents and teachers do—they're training a child's mind. And this is all the more reason why the field of parenting is a hot topic for researchers. Countless books have been written on the topic of parenting, and several seminars and workshops conducted.

While we are all part of the modern, globalized world, can we still learn about parenting from our ancient Indian wisdom?

Yes. And in this matter, Chanakya is a master of child psychology.

His method of raising a child is time-tested and relevant to every generation.

'For the first five years, love your child unconditionally, for the next ten years, discipline him. From the sixteenth year onwards, treat him as a friend.' (3.18)

No other person could have summed up parenting in such a beautiful and easy-to-understand manner. In two lines, Chanakya gives us a frame that parents, especially new parents, can work with.

Till five years

When children are born, they require a lot of love and care. Even the mistakes of a child bring joy because a child doesn't ever intend to make them. Every child is a representation of God. The spark of divinity can be found in everything a child does—the way it plays around, the way it struggles with its new world, how it's constantly trying to make sense of things.

So, while raising your child, for the first five years you must give it unconditional love and care. Do not expect the child to understand the ways of the world. Instead, you need to understand the ways of the child.

The instruction given is to love the child 'unconditionally'. Whatever the child does, accept it as it is. Even if the child breaks the most precious object in the house or hits back at you, love it unconditionally. Accept it with joy. There is nothing you can achieve by beating the child in order to discipline him.

The worst child abuse cases happen in this age group. So, family members have to deal with the children in a sensitive manner. Remember, children brought up with love and care will always feel needed and wanted wherever they go.

For the next ten years

The second stage of parenting is for the next ten years—from ages six to fifteen. This is the time to discipline them.

Now, the logic of the child has developed. It can think independently. It now has a capacity for reasoning and wants to enquire more. There are various famous books like the 'Tell Me Why?' series for children, if you'd like to read more on this topic. So, as you are feeding them with information, make sure they also get used to a word called 'No'.

Disciplining the child is a very important point of parenting. Swami Chinmayananda put it nicely, 'For the healthy development of a child, you require the love of the mother and the discipline of the father.'

If a child is not corrected at this phase of life, then it is at the risk of picking up bad behaviour that'll be even harder to correct later in life. Remember, in this phase of life the child is growing physically and mentally at super speed. Speed, if not directed properly, can cause accidents.

Now, disciplining does not mean beating a child. You can discipline them at a mental level. Create a healthy fear in the mind of the child that prevents it from taking things for granted.

After sixteen years

When the child becomes a young adult, your parenting role is over.

We forget that parenting is a role, and not one's identity. The child grows out of its childhood, but parents never grow out of parenting.

Remember, we are bringing up human beings. They will be on their own one day. In fact, that is the whole point— to raise strong, independent children who are comfortable leaving you one day and can build their own lives. The end of their dependency will be a success on your part. So from the sixteenth year onwards, start considering them as your friends.

Now they are on equal terms with you. Both of you should be able to discuss any topic with ease. And you'll find that you can actually learn a lot from them.

Kahlil Gibran put it well in his book, *The Prophet*:

Your children are not your children.
They are the sons and daughters of Life's longing for itself.
They come through you but not from you,
And though they are with you, yet they belong not to you.

57

Women's Rights

THE WORD 'RIGHTS' is usually understood as a legal term.

And when it comes to 'women's rights', the discourse includes women's equality, women's liberation and gender neutrality around the world.

But let us look at this from a totally different angle. In Indian culture, the world 'right' is connected to the word 'duty'.

So, one person's duty is another person's right. And someone's right is the duty of another person. So, if one fulfils his duty, the right of another person is automatically taken care of. If each person fulfils his or her responsibility, then there is no need to demand rights.

Let me explain with a few examples.

It is the duty of parents to look after their kids, take care of them and educate them. It is the right of a child to be taken care of and to receive proper education. Now, if the parent's duty is to bring up the child and educate him properly, the child need not demand his 'right to education'. It is already provided for.

Similarly, it is the duty of the young generation to take care of the elders in their house. And it is the right of the elders to be taken care of by the young generation in their old age. So, if the young generation performs its duty properly, the rights of the elders are automatically taken care of.

It is very interesting to see the connection between 'duty' and 'rights'.

Now, in this chapter, let us understand what are the rights of women in the family, To put it another way, what is the duty of the men towards the women in the family?

Chanakya says,

'Maintenance and ornaments constitute women's property.'
(3.2.14)

A woman has the right over her maintenance and ornaments.

It is interesting that this is mentioned in the *Arthashastra* because it is relevant even today across the globe. Even in the case of divorce, the concept of alimony is given a legal status. Alimony is the spousal maintenance, a legal obligation on a person to provide financial support to his spouse before or after marital separation or divorce.

It is not just a legal but also the moral responsibility of male members of the family to give maintenance money to the women in the house. Chanakya had even suggested that the king should pay the queen and his mother maintenance charges.

When it comes to ornaments, they have to be given to the women without a doubt. After all, they love jewellery.

How do we practise this in our families?

Women and money

Irrespective of the woman being an earning member of the family or not, she has a right to her maintenance. She may not demand it, but the males have to pay for it. After all, whatever you give to a woman, she will only multiply and give it back to you.

Once there was a working couple. The wife was earning more than the husband. But every month the husband used to give her pocket money. She would say jokingly, 'My money is my money. His money is also mine.'

There is a very important connection between women and money. They understand it better than men. In our tradition, we have given wealth a form of Goddess Laxmi.

The shopping habit

There is another dimension about money and women. Money is used for shopping. But note that a women will not just shop for herself, she will also shop and buy goods for the whole family. She thinks holistically. She will buy groceries and make a meal for everyone. She will buy curtains and decorative items and convert your house into a home.

So shopping is not a self-centred activity for a woman. Allow her to shop. She also knows something interesting—how to save. Even the poorest woman will save for her family and children. While she spends, she also knows when and where to stop. Understanding of economics is a natural gift for her.

The love for ornaments

Women have a natural affinity for beauty. Aesthetics and appreciation of art is innate to them. Therefore, the love for ornaments is part of a lady's personality.

She uses ornaments to wear and display her personality. But it is also something she will let go of if a situation demands it. A woman will sell off her most favourite ornament when a need or crisis arises.

So give the freedom to the ladies of the house to decide what is good for them.

Once we have understood this as being our duty towards them, we have understood Indian culture in the right manner.

58

Respect in the Family

IT IS NOT enough to exist in a family. One needs to contribute to it.

Every person goes through three stages in life—dependent, independent and interdependent. In the first stage, which is when we're children, we are totally dependent on our families for our very survival.

Then comes the stage of independence. This is when the child becomes a teenager or a young adult. At this point it wants nothing more than to be free. It wants to move out and make a mark for itself.

The final stage is that of interdependence. In this stage the person gets married and settles down and becomes a parent. The person feels that all they need is their family. And they realize the value of their grandparents because it is them who'll help raise the child. Grandparents are instrumental in passing on family values. When we reach this stage we understand that grandparents, parents and children all need each other, and are interdependent.

Those who understand this principle will always find a way to harmonize with everybody and will be respected by every member of their family.

Chanakya had said that if an individual does not have a purpose in life, he will never be respected.

He said,

'A person who has no faith, no wealth, no love and no salvation goes on taking birth and dying without any purpose.' (CN 3.20)

So, the secret to earn the respect of your family is to contribute in some way or the other.

How do we use Chanakya's advice from the above verse? Here's how:

Faith in family tradition

Every family has a tradition, a parampara. There are some unwritten rules within the family which are practised by every member. For example, we touch our elders' feet to show them respect, as well as take their blessings.

You should be actively involved in the activities in your family. Poojas, weddings of relatives, birthdays, house-warming ceremonies are all part of every family and you should always be present at such occasions.

You may initially not understand the gravity of these little actions, but do it anyway. You will slowly gain the respect of not just your family members but of your community too.

Contribute financially

Finances play a huge role in every family. You must contribute financially as per your capacity, more so when you are part of a joint family. Taking care of household expenses like food and grocery, electricity, etc. will never go unappreciated. Make sure you do your bit as an earning member.

It is not necessary that you have to give a large sum of money to prove your importance in the family. Even small gestures matter. In the Ramayana, while building the bridge to Lanka, the squirrels and the monkeys took a rock each to help build the bridge. It was their way of expressing their love. Similarly, your love too will shine through in the simplest of gestures.

Show a purpose

There are some members of the family who may not be as productive as the others. Usually, some members like the old people, the unmarried dependent relatives, or the non-earning members tend to feel less confident because they're not contributing monetarily. But they needn't feel inferior about themselves.

Such people too are capable of contributing in a significant manner. They just need to create a purpose for themselves and their family. They could spend more time with children, help them with their studies and pass on values to them through storytelling. They can take care of the household chores or run other errands. Point being that each and every person is capable of making themselves useful at home.

And in this manner, when each person does his or her bit, there is a sense of mutual respect in the family.

59

Common Property

WITHIN A FAMILY there are two kinds of properties—individual property and common property.

What is individual property? A house that you bought, your own investments in bonds, shares, etc. These are your personal assets. No other person can lay claim on them and you have the final say on matters related to them.

What is common property? Something that belongs to all members of the family. It could be an ancestral home, a temple in the village that was built by your forefathers, or a piece of uncultivated land. These are family assets and decisions regarding these are made by consulting all the members of the family.

In this chapter, we are going to discuss what is to be done with common property.

A wise person once said, 'Build your individual property and protect your common property.'

But sometimes people do the reverse. They never build

any individual property with their own hard work and efforts. Rather, they think the common property is their individual property and fight over it.

This spells disaster for the whole family. No one wants to make something of their own. Instead of contributing something to the new generation, they feed off of the old, eventually destroying it in the process.

So Chanakya decided to enlighten us on the subject and help us never go astray. He says,

> 'By mutual agreement, one may get things done as desired, (and) should avoid what is undesirable.' (3.8.18)

The main ingredient in any good relationship is mutual agreement. The same applies to family members.

First of all, there has to be mutual respect among all the members. A difference of opinion need not corrode one's respect for the other. The head of the family has to take everyone's interests into account; this is his or her role as a leader.

So, if there is a discussion about common property, these are the steps to be followed:

Call a meeting

In matters related to the common property of your family, never take decisions alone, even if you can. It's simply not your place to do so.

So, if you're considering selling off your ancestral property, you must call a family meeting. Regardless of whether the property has been neglected or remains unused for decades or is in some remote village. You must take everyone's opinion into account and arrive at a consensus before taking any decisions.

We don't realize this but we're sometimes literally one impulsive decision away from ruining a relationship. So Chanakya's advice is to always act *with* the family, and not on *behalf* of them.

Listen to all

It is not necessary that everyone will share the same point of view on everything, least of all where the common property is concerned. Some may have an emotional attachment to the place as it belongs to their ancestors, and would think of it as their only remaining connection to the past. While others may look at from a practical angle and only see the financial gains to be made.

Some might even want to redevelop the property into a resort to maximize their revenue and have a steady inflow of money. Whatever be their thoughts, we need to hear them out. Everyone must be allowed a chance to voice their opinion on the matter before you arrive at an informed and unanimous decision.

Consult the wise

Finally, revere your elders, for their wisdom is something that can only be earned with time. Their inputs are critical in this matter, because they did the most to contribute to the family. The younger generation will offer one perspective while the older one would offer a completely different one. Whatever it may be, listening to both sides will help you have a well-rounded approach to the matter. Your decision could be totally different from what it actually started out as. So, be open to out-of-the-box solutions in such matters.

There was once a common family property that was lying idle for a long time. None of the relatives had any emotional connection to the ancestral property and mutually decided to sell it. There was no dispute or fight. They even signed a legal agreement.

But then something strange happened. When one of the children from that family went there for the first time, she was emotionally touched by the property. The father of the girl finally bought the property himself.

All the relatives were also happy. Instead of selling it to an outsider, the property remained within the family. Plus, the ownership was also clearly defined.

In terms of common property, this situation is a win-win.

60

Irresponsible to Responsible

FAMILY LIFE HAS its own ups and down.

It is like travelling in a valley. When you are travelling, the roads go up and down and there are unexpected turns. So, too, is the case with families.

There are happy moments and sad moments. There are moments when we feel totally frustrated and ask ourselves, 'Why did I ever get married? It was so nice to be single and all alone.'

But the grass will always be greener on the other side of the fence. The unmarried feel that it is better to get married. They feel the absence of that one person who will always take care of them, or who they can count on at all times. So, in reality, it'll always be a mixed bag of emotions. Good times along with the bad. But we often start envying the other side when we feel the weight of responsibilities on our shoulders.

When family responsibility becomes difficult to handle, and the husband especially feels dejected, he may experience a strong urge to run away from home. It is easy to run away from one's responsibilities. But that is not a solution. Whatever be the problem, one has to face it.

Chanakya believed that anyone who abandons their family and doesn't fulfil his duties towards his family should be punished.

In the *Arthashastra*, such irresponsible behaviour is considered a crime.

In the 'Dharmasthiya', which deals with the subject of law in the *Arthashastra*, this is the punishment suggested for such a runaway, irresponsible person:

> **'As between a father and son, husband and wife, brother and sister, maternal uncle and nephew, or teacher and pupil, for the one abandoning the other and going away, the fine for violence shall be the punishment.' (3.20.18)**

Every relationship comes with its set of responsibilities. But some relationships are to be honoured no matter what. And in such relationships, one cannot take the other person for granted or run away when the time comes to fulfil one's duties, no matter how hard that may be.

There are examples of such relationships that Chanakya gives in the above sutra. Between a father and a son—this is one where there is always a generation gap. The father may assume that the son is not mature enough. And his attitude may translate into the son feeling that his father does not trust him at all.

Between a husband and a wife—differences of opinion is inevitable in such an equation. Two individuals are bound to think differently and sometimes they might inadvertently end up adding different dimensions to the same problem. Couple this with a lack of mutual respect, and you're looking at a huge fight.

Brother and sister, or it can be between two brothers, or two sisters—siblings have their share of heated moments. But it should not result in sibling rivalry.

Maternal uncle and nephew—this is another important relation in a family. The brother of your mother, your maternal uncle, is as good as your own father. The way you have a responsibility towards your father, you have a similar responsibility towards your mother's family too.

Teacher and pupil—the student has a lifelong duty towards his teacher and his gurukul. Obeying his instructions and following in his footsteps is the highest responsibility for a pupil.

So, what does one do during frustrating moments in their relationships?

Take a break

It is easy to run away. It is easy to say 'It is not my problem'. It is easy to feel that if you're not around, someone else will take care of them. But it is not a part of our Indian culture to be selfish.

If there has been a fight, that is fine. Just relax. Reflect over it. Take a break. Do not take any decisions in anger. Sometimes the best decision is not to take a decision. Allow some time to pass before you respond to the situation.

Solutions will emerge

There was a person who, in midst of the most difficult

situations, always kept his cool. Someone asked him, 'How come you remain so calm and quiet all the time?' With a smile he said, 'When the problem comes to me face-to-face, I mentally tell the problem to come the next day. I like to go to sleep without thinking of the problem.'

He continued, 'Next morning the solution comes to me without effort. I do not know how, but it has always worked.'

Similarly, when it boils down to a tense situation in your families, do not react. Wait. Let some time pass. And then respond.

And, as the person said, the solution will come on its own.

61

Charity Begins at Home

CHARITY BEGINS AT home.

There is a practice in Indian culture called 'danam', meaning giving to charity. It is a quality that every person should develop, according to Lord Krishna in the Bhagwad Gita (chapter 16, verse 1).

We have always been told to share our wealth. Nothing belongs to you alone, be it money, food or knowledge. Give it and it will come back to you tenfold.

The wealthy people who are respected by everyone are not those who simply make money, but those who share their wealth and knowledge with others.

So, when is the right time to give? Right here and right now!

That does not mean one should give impulsively. You need to think through and give. Is it for a worthy cause? Is it for the right person? One is better off giving after taking these things into account.

Chanakya says that you should not delay too much in giving, because the harsh truth is that you never know when death will come for you.

'**While the body is healthy and work worthy and death is away, one must do charity and good deeds. When death comes there will be no time left to do anything.**' (CN 4.4)

One need not wait until old age to give to charity. One should develop the habit of giving in one's youth itself. When your body is healthy and you get an opportunity to contribute your strength, physical and mental, to a worthy cause—give.

It is not necessary that you need to only dedicate yourself to a selfless cause. Sometimes, it's important to be generous to oneself. After all, you are your biggest cause. Because when death comes to take you, you won't have any more time left to give. And as you know, death will take away everything you created in this lifetime. Except for your meritorious deeds, everything else dies with you.

Give small and big

How much should you give? That is for you to decide. It can be as per your capacity and inclination. If you can't afford big, then give small. If you can afford big, then surely give big. But give.

The best way to teach children the value of charity is to lead by example. Whenever you give, make sure they are around. So, for instance, when you take the child to a temple or a church, and you find the donation box, instead of putting in money yourself, ask your child to put the money in the box.

In this simple manner, you introduce the child to the act of giving. Then during their birthdays, make sure that part of the allowance being spent on the party goes to charity. I know of a child who developed the habit of giving food to orphans on his birthday. She said, 'I can feed my friends any time of the year. But at least during birthdays let me share happiness with the less-fortunate children.'

Plan a charity

There is another method of giving. You can plan your charity. You can raise a fund that encourages people to donate a small percentage of their earnings for charity, say 10 per cent, and then give away the money for some social causes.

A family once made a separate account just for charity. Each family member contributed to it. They first created the fund, and then were on a lookout for worthy causes to donate the money. But then they ran into a financial crisis and did not have enough money to pay the month's bills. No money, save for the charity fund.

They decided to borrow money from that fund temporarily. When things came back to normal, they put back the money they had borrowed into the fund. The lady of the house said, 'That was God's money that helped us in the time of crisis. Now we have to give it back to him.'

The other side

There is a notion that charity is only for the poor and needy sections of the society. Of course they should be helped. But that does not mean others do not require our financial help.

There are many worthy causes on the other side of society. Artists, scientists, sportspersons—they all require some form of financial support or assistance, depending on their economic backgrounds.

A poor child may require money for his healthcare and education; a scientist may require money for his next research; an artist may need money to buy the things he needs to help create art; a sportsman may need sponsorship to buy safety gear that are essential for him to practise his sport. If encouraged, each of these people are capable of achieving their dreams. All they need is a little push.

62

Books at Home

HOW MANY BOOKS do you have at home?

Now that is a direct question from this bestselling author.

You may find this a bit strange that this chapter comes under the 'family' section, but it is very relevant here. Do you know that I have over 5,000 books at home, and the number is only growing.

You may think that there is a lot of space in my house and therefore, I can afford to keep these books. But it is not a question of space. It is a question of love for books and love for knowledge. Even though, by the grace of God, I have a decently big house where I can manage to keep so many books, every few years my house gets overloaded with books and I have to either make a new shelf or shift them somewhere else.

The idea is that as a nation we do not dedicate a good amount of space for books in our homes. How many of us plan for a library in our houses when we buy them? We plan for a kitchen, hall and bedroom. But how about a study-room?

I have travelled across the globe and found that in some countries it is part of their culture to have a library at home. We have to build such a culture in our country—a place especially for books.

It is my parents who developed the habit in our family to read and have lots of books around. My wife and I continue that tradition. Interestingly, without much effort, even our children have developed a love for books. So reading books has become a family tradition.

It is not that I became an author first and then started collecting books. It is the other way around. I became an author because I loved collecting and reading books.

So welcome to the field of knowledge.

Chanakya said,

> 'Knowledge is like a holy Kamadhenu cow.
> It bears fruit in all seasons. In foreign lands it protects
> and rewards. That is why it is considered inbuilt secret
> treasure.' (CN 4.5)

Kamadhenu is a cow mentioned in the Indian scriptures. It is believed to have given endless streams of milk and fulfilled everyone's wishes. So is the case with investing in knowledge. It gives us endless returns.

There is a famous saying—give a man a fish, he will eat for one time. Teach him how to fish, and he will eat for the rest of his life. Therefore, the aim is to build a family that is so knowledgeable that no crisis can stop it.

Share and exchange

Every person in the family has different sets of experiences and is knowledgeable on different subjects. We may be working in different professions, and hence would have knowhow in different fields. Even someone at home, like a homemaker, would have knowledge of how to cook food and manage the whole family.

Whatever it is, share your knowledge and experience with others in your family. A mother can teach her kids how to cook. Gone are the days when only the girls and ladies would cook. A boy is expected to know how to cook. He can then survive in any part of the world.

If the father works in an office or factory, he can share his work experience with others. It is not right to think that such knowledge is only helpful in one's professional matters. Others in the family can also learn a lot from it.

Your understanding

Every person has a different understanding of what s/he does. Communicate the same to others. For example, take up a small fun project in your family where you exchange book reviews. If there are four members, let each of them read and study a different topic or a book. Let each person make a presentation of their 'book review' in front of the others.

You can share your understanding from the book and its topics. It will broaden your understanding of the other person from your family and vice versa.

Love and wisdom

Love and knowledge go hand-in-hand in a family. One develops with the other.

It is said that there used to be a Sufi saint who read books to everyone in the family. Some neighbours also started coming to listen to him during the book-reading time. One day, he had a sore throat and could not read out loud to the others. His wife took the book and started reading. Her understanding of the subject surprised everybody. They said his wife was wiser than him.

So, you never know whom you are influencing when you gather and distribute your wealth of knowledge.

63

Managing Your Servants

YOUR SERVANTS ARE the pillars of your household.

Ask anyone who works. Without the support of the domestic help, people would not be able to work peacefully and productively at office or even at home.

Today, the word servant itself has been replaced with the more positive-sounding 'help'. It is now being considered as a very dignified job. And rightfully so. We need to respect them for what they do, for without them, work in our own households would come to a standstill.

But it is also important to maintain discipline, because sometimes they tend to take you for granted.

Studies have proven that paying employees a high salary is not enough to ensure productivity.

So Chanakya knows the method to make the helpers at home productive.

He says,

'A wage is for work done, not for what is not done.'
(3.14.8)

Pay your servants well. But pay them only for the work they have done. If they do not work, do not pay them. Now, this may come across as a very strict statement. But the idea is not to be cruel; it is to send a message that work is to be respected. And also the money you give is to be respected.

So, how does one balance discipline and love with servants?

Here are a few steps we can follow:

Define the work

Our equation with our house help is a simple give-and-take one. They offer their services and we pay them for it. Workers are usually classified as unskilled, semi-skilled, skilled and highly skilled, as per industry standards. So ideally, a worker should be paid as per the skills he has.

So, make sure you clarify exactly what work is to be done and are on the same page as your domestic help on this matter. Is the helper trained and comes with previous experience? If required, do a reference check on the person and his or her previous background.

A mutual agreement of the tasks to be fulfilled is a good way of avoiding future problems.

Agree on the wage

Mostly the workers of this category start with a daily wage agreement. The daily wages depend on various factors—the kind of work, the city or village where they are working, the skills, the experience, the rates prevalent in the market, etc. Some associations and government bodies even define a minimum daily wage structure.

If required, also look into the legal aspect of this. Because the law makes it mandatory for us to make sure the people who work for us are rightly paid. Their safety is also our responsibility.

During the agreement it is also important to define what you will 'not' pay for. This helps avoid unrealistic expectations altogether.

Watch and be human

You can't always go by the rulebook. After a person has started working for you, watch the person carefully. In the initial stages, you will have to train and support him. Do that with human concern. Your servants are not your slaves. They are also human beings, and require some time to adjust to you, just as you do to adjust to them.

Watch their sincerity at work. Trust them enough to fulfil their duty. Respect them enough and they will work sincerely for you.

If a person works for you over a long period, then you have to become more flexible. Give them regular salaries, leaves and even other support. There have been many cases where the servant has so much devotion towards the family that they become family members.

In fact, the children in such households don't treat them as servants, but as uncles and aunts.

And why shouldn't they? After all, they are more than servants. They are people you can rely on.

64

Company of the Noble

THIS WORLD IS full of challenges.

Every person has his or her own challenges. The student's challenge is to pass the exams; the businessman's challenge is to secure himself financially, the politician's challenge is to run a nation.

So too when you get married. As a spouse you face a different set of challenges.

But after having faced all the challenges of the world, you only look forward to coming home if it is a place that offers some relief. If not, then your house is also a living hell.

There are some people who stay back late at office just to spend less time at home. Or they may leave office but instead of going home and spending time with their family, they purposefully go to a different place and delay going home. For such people, even a weekend is exhausting.

Why does this happen? It is because there is no peace at home. On the contrary, they feel disturbed when they are at home. And hence, they'd rather spend time outside.

Chanakya knew that few things are bound to make any person happy at home.

He pointed out,

'In this world, the hell of miseries, only three things provide some cool relief, good offspring, a devoted wife and the company of the noble people.' (CN 4.10)

The world is full of miseries. The sheer struggle a person faces is enough to mentally burn him out. So, there must be some relief that awaits him when he comes home. Chanakya says that good children, a good wife and the company of noble people, these three are all the saviours we need.

When a person comes home tired and looks forward to meeting his family, he is already a happy man. Being greeted by a welcoming wife and smiling children makes his day's stress and tension vanish. The same is applicable for the working woman today. When she comes home and her husband and children welcome her, she feels relieved.

There is one more way of always keeping yourself and your family happy—the company of the noble. This is called 'sat-sangh' in Sanskrit. 'Sat' is noble and 'sangh' is company.

When you have noble people coming to your house regularly, your house draws good energy from them.

How do we have such people visiting you and making your place a happy home?

The teachers

There are many teachers in our life. They could be our

schoolteachers, spiritual teachers or even our elderly relatives. Try to spend some time with them on a daily basis. Their noble thoughts will change your life. Such people provide us with a sense of direction in our life, even during the worst of times.

As you go to meet them, make sure you invite them to your place too. Organize a lunch or dinner. Make sure all your family members listen to their words of wisdom. If possible, gather the people around and ask them to speak about their life experiences. They can give you a lot of insight about how to lead a noble life yourself.

Tuesdays with Morrie

Have you heard about this famous book named *Tuesdays with Morrie*? This book is not to be missed. Written by an American writer, Mitch Albom, it narrates the author's story of going to meet his old teacher. He finds out that the teacher, Morrie Schwartz, is dying. And he decides to go every Tuesday and listen to his teacher.

He goes for fourteen Tuesdays and records all the conversations. And the teacher gives him his life's greatest lessons before passing away. The book captures all the messages, which everyone can practise in life.

Do you have a teacher, a Morrie, in your life? Then do not wait for him or her to reach their deathbed to get all the wisdom. Do it right now.

A weekly schedule

Make appointments with noble people. You can plan a weekly schedule with them. Take your family along. There are many places where such people give spiritual discourses and share their noble ideas.

They can be found everywhere, in temples, mosques, churches and other spiritual places. They are present in the ashrams all around. Find a place close by and visit. There are some clubs like Rotary and Lions Clubs that also help us reach such people who are doing noble work for society.

When we associate ourselves with such people and become part of their lives, then not just us, even our family benefits.

The journey starts with meeting a noble person, and ends with making the whole family noble and happy.

65

Family Trips

LIFE HAS BECOME hectic.

A family hardly gets any time to spend with each other.

Life was a lot more easygoing before technology took over families. But if the parents are busy working, the children are busy with school, and grandparents are busy with their priorities, what is the best way to connect with each other? A family trip! It's the perfect break from one's regular routine life, plus everyone enjoys such an outing. The most excited lot are the children.

Now, the family trips may not be just for fun and frolic. They can be a good way to educate your children beyond the schoolbooks.

Chanakya has clearly said that parents should instruct children on values,

> 'Therefore he should instruct him in what conduces spiritual and material good.' (1.17.33)

The suggestion given here is that as parents, we need to give our children two types of instructions—what is spiritually good and what is materially good. In other words, we need to teach them spiritual values and moral values. And also, at the same time, we need to teach them the importance of being materially successful.

You could use Chanakya's advice during your next family trip and here's how:

Planning a family trip

It is so much fun when you plan a family trip together. Make it a group activity with your family members. Ask them which places they'd like to go to. Let them do some research on the Internet. Find some good locations, book tickets and hotels. Shop for the trip. All this is fun.

Doing this together helps strengthen the bond between you and your family.

Time with kids

During the trip, spend some time with kids. You can tell them about your experiences in life. Share stories of your childhood. Also tell them the importance of the places you are visiting.

One thing to remember—do not be a miser during the whole trip. You should allocate a budget for the trip. It is not suggested that you indulge and overspend. Sometimes cost-cutting in some matters destroys the fun of the trip.

Make a project

After you come back home, do not think the trip is over.

Give the children a chance to recollect the whole trip. Ask them to write down what they learnt from the trip. This way, even though the trip will be over, the things they learn on the trip will remain for life. Also show them an account of the money you spent during the trip. This is the best way of teaching them about finances. Here on out, they will be looking forward to the next trip.

As the Chinese saying goes, 'A person learns more from a day's travel, than from reading a hundred books.'

66

Chanakya's Seven Pillars of a Family

EVERY FAMILY STRUCTURE (for example, a joint family, a nuclear family) is based on certain principles.

In India, a joint family is a known structure. While in the West, a nuclear family or single parent family is quite normal.

Chanakya was a great strategist who believed in going about things methodically. He has suggested a great structure to follow that'll help you strengthen your family.

There is a famous saptanga model of Chanakya, which was used by various kings for running their kingdoms effectively.

We can use this saptanga model for creating a good family structure too.

So, let us first understand what this saptanga model given by Chanakya is all about. He said,

'Swami, Amatya, Janapad, Durg, Kosha, Dand, Mitra—iti Prakritraya.' (6.1.1)

'The king, the minister, the citizens, the fortified city, the treasury, the army and the allies—these are the constituent elements of the state.'

Chanakya says that there are seven things that go into making of a good kingdom. The king has to ensure that all these seven things are in place. Then the kingdom will be an example of the perfect kingdom.

So what are these seven essential components of a kingdom? The king himself, along with efficient ministers, good citizens, living in a good infrastructure (like a fortified city), along with good finances, protected from enemies by an army, and supported by good allies.

Chanakya says iti prakriti (the nature) of the kingdom is based on these seven parts.

The same model can be used to create the perfect family.

Here's an interpretation of the above sutra that you can use:

Swami—The head of the family

The head of the family is a very important person. He takes full responsibility for the family. Usually this person's main job is to keep the family together. As children we may not understand the sacrifices the head makes to run the family. Even the financial needs are taken care of by this head.

Amatya—The life partner

This is the spouse. Without the spouse the family cannot function. The spouse is as important as the head of the family because their contribution is significant. The family knows that the whole maintenance and sustenance is dependent on the spouse. Amatya is the second-in-charge of the family. Without the Amatya, the swami is incomplete.

Janapad—The children

There could be a husband and a wife. But the family will feel incomplete without children. They bring joy into the household. They are the very heart and essence of a family. There are many couples who adopt children when they cannot conceive. Because children teach us unconditional love. They are mirrors to our soul.

Durg—The house

The family requires shelter to live. Like I said earlier, it is a family that turns a house into a home.

In the beginning we can have a small house. But, as the family keeps growing, we may require a bigger house. It is always better to own a house than rent it. After all, this house is not just a temporary place to stay; this is where our souls long to come.

Kosha—The finance

Money is required to run the house. Without the right finances in place, it is impossible to pay bills, buy groceries and maintain a household, let alone bring up children. As long as the finances are sorted out, there is peace in the house. If not, fights are rather common. So, financial stability is a very important aspect of making a happy family.

Danda—Your support system/relatives

Our relatives are our biggest support system. They fulfil our emotional requirements too. Our cousins, uncles and aunts, grandparents, in-laws, are the very reason we call ourselves a family. They also come to our rescue now and then.

Mitra—The friends

Your friends become part of your family. Even though they may not be related to you, they are connected to you at a deeper level. In many cases friends are grow even closer than the family. Your neighbours could fall in this category, because of their constant presence and support.

Even if one of the seven pillars is missing, there's bound to be strain in such a family. When all the seven are in place, we know that no power in the world can break this family.

Family Succession

YOU HAVE DONE your bit.

As a family person, your duties have been fulfilled. Your children are grown up and now you are happily living a retired life. You're probably a grandparent too.

Now, there is one last duty in your life that you need to fulfil—it concerns your family succession. Who will be the head of your family after you? Suppose you have a large business, which of the family members will you choose as your heir?

The general assumption is that the eldest son will take over the headship of the family and will head the family business too.

However, Chanakya disagrees. If the son is capable, then this option works. But what if he does not show the capability?

Chanakya warns,

'He should not install on the throne an only son, if undisciplined.' (1.17.51)

Think of the situation given above. The king has an only son. He is obviously bound to be attached to his son. But then the son is totally undisciplined. Chanakya advises the king against making such a son his successor.

Love for your children can make you blind to their faults. And it may happen that you will make a child your successor regardless of whether s/he will justice to the position or not.

The classic example is of the Mahabharata. Dhritarashta, the king and the father of the Kauravas, fell into the same trap. He was already physically blind, but his love for his sons made him intellectually blind too. His sense of judgement was flawed.

Duryodhana, his cruel son, was given the power. In spite of wise people like Bhishma and Vidura warning Dhritarashta, he did not listen.

And what was the end result? The Mahabharata war took place. The whole family got destroyed and finally all the sons were killed.

So learn from history. Follow the advice of Chanakya as far as succession planning is concerned:

Benefit of all

Do not look at seniority as the only criterion of capability. Rama, the eldest son of Dasharatha, the king of Ayodhya, was very capable. But it's not necessary that every elder child is like Rama. Sometimes the youngest child may be more capable. So keep a keen eye on your children to see who has got leadership qualities in them.

Chanakya gives a tip on how to identify a leader among your children. 'Those who see the benefit of all.' Meaning, the child who is thinking of the welfare of his people is the right leader for your family. Your successor should have a large heart and broad shoulders—a large heart to accommodate the mistakes of other family members, and a broad shoulder to take the responsibilities that comes with leadership.

It can be a girl

Why is it that only the son can be the successor? That is not fair. There have been many instances in the past where when kings were looking for their successor, they did not find their sons suitable. They, in turn, made the capable women in their family the next leaders. Travancore kingdom, now part of Kerala state, has various examples of female rulers. The queen of Jhansi and Ahilyabai Holkar from Indore are other examples. They were highly successful and respected leaders.

Girls should be given the same freedom as boys. They are naturally good at multitasking, which is an essential quality for leadership. And the ability to manage work and family is something that comes naturally to them.

Think long term

Lord Krishna says in the Mahabharata, 'While taking a decision today, think what history will talk about you.' We need to weigh the impact of our decisions on our future. When we do think of the long term, we start looking at our family from a totally different light.

Some decisions are tough in the initial stage. Also, others may not understand your logic behind those decisions. But if you have done all your calculations right, then go ahead and follow your gut to choose the next big leader. Do not hesitate.

While choosing the heir to the Magadha kingdom, Chanakya carefully chose a boy from a poor family, Chandragupta Maurya. Not many agreed with him at the time when he started to train Chandragupta. But Chanakya had already seen the spark of leadership in the boy.

Today, Chandragupta Maurya is listed among the greatest kings of India, all over the world.

68

Private Space

A FAMILY IS a group. But that group comprises a set of individuals who have their own independent interests.

Let us not forget one important aspect of life—even though we need each other in our lives, we also need our own private space.

Offering some their silent time and space is another way of showing your respect to them.

To respect one another's individuality, we must also never compare people with each other. The very fact that one is an individual implies that they are born 'unique'. When we compare our child with another, indirectly we're sending a message to our child that they are not as good as the other.

So, if your child is not doing well in studies, do not compare him or her with others who are excelling in studies. Yes, you could help your child improve and get better grades. But constantly pressure him and you will end up denting his self-confidence for sure. Instead, try and find out what your child is good at and let him immerse himself in those creative pursuits. So, without mutual respect for every individual member of your family, life will become a living hell.

Chanakya goes to the extent of saying that you should quit such a family and go away. He said,

'A man must quit a religion that does not preach love and kindness. Similarly one should leave a teacher who has no knowledge to impart, a person who has a short temper and relatives who have no love to give.' (CN 4.16)

According to Chanakya, these are things you should quit—a religion or a philosophy that does not preach love, kindness and mutual respect; a teacher who has no knowledge; a short-tempered person.

And as for family, quit those relatives who do not love you.

The suggestion is a positive one. It's better to be surrounded by relatives who love you. And the best way to encourage this sort of harmony is to give everyone the space they deserve.

How does one develop that?

Do not disturb

There are people who keep disturbing others continuously. They talk to you even if you seem disinterested. Such a person is bound to be disliked. So each member of the family should know when another member has mentally put on the 'Do not disturb' sign. There is a wise saying, 'Do not give advice until it is asked for, otherwise there will be no value for the advice given.' Only reach out when needed.

Listen

We should develop the habit of listening to our family members. Listening is not just hearing. It is hearing plus thinking. When people talk, it is not necessary they mean what they say. So, try to read between the lines. A person may just have had a very bad day and therefore may be expressing his or her anger. So, do not get upset if they are harsh towards you. It may not be directed at you at all.

Be patient with them. By allowing them to express their feelings, you are letting them know that you understand their situation and will be there for them whenever they need you.

Let go

Often we are over-protective of our children and younger family members because we love them so much. It's okay to be concerned about them. That's healthy and compassionate behaviour. But if we start worrying about them all the time, we will end up pushing them away and create a negative atmosphere at home. If you're worried they'll fail, let them. Let them learn on their own. After all, everyone has their own life's lessons to learn. It is always better to let go of our children when they are ready. Remember, you cannot teach them everything. They have to learn some things on their own and from others too.

People are like butterflies. If you chase them, they will fly away. If you just allow them to be free, they will come and sit next to you.

Remember, true love is always without attachment.

69

Feeling of Gratitude

'THANK YOU.'

It is a simple yet powerful phrase if uttered genuinely.

In life one will have many ups and downs, highs and lows. But if one learns to be grateful, then one will always find happiness.

What is the best way to develop a feeling of gratitude? The simple answer is prayer.

Prayer doesn't mean begging God for something. It is a way of expressing thankfulness to God at every point of life. When do we pray to God? Only in distress? No. One should pray in good times and bad, in the beginning and also at the end.

Chanakya, one of the most intelligent strategists, also believed in the power of prayers. He knew there is an intelligence higher than human intelligence. So, when you invoke the lord, you automatically get blessed with the power and wisdom needed to do any important work in life.

Therefore, while starting to write his greatest book, the

Arthashastra, the first and the foremost thing Chanakya did was to pray and invoke the great teachers.

The first opening line of the *Arthashastra* of Chanakya starts with a prayer,

'Om Namah Sukra Brihaspati-abyam.'
'Om. Salutations to Sukra and Brihaspati.'

'Om' is not just a word or a sound. It holds within the knowledge of the universe. Om has over a hundred meanings. One of them is a welcome to the gods. Therefore, we start all prayers with Om.

Sukra and Brihaspati were ancient acharyas in the field of political science. These two great masters had written their own arthashastras (books) on politics and raja-niti. Chanakya himself, as a student, had studied the work of these two wise men. While writing his *Arthashastra*, Chanakya remembered them and other teachers who guided him along the way. He prayed to them, expressing his gratitude, and only then did he start penning down his thoughts.

Usually, when we write a book or an article—or anything for that matter—many of us do not acknowledge the previous writers who may have inspired us. This is not good. Give credit to those who rightfully deserve it. Chanakya teaches us this essential value we must all have—to express our gratitude towards those who inspired us and were part of our journey in some way.

So what can we all do on a daily basis to develop this healthy attitude? Here's what:

Your family

No family is perfect. Every family has its own set of strengths and weaknesses. But instead of looking at what is missing in your family, you should be focusing on what you have. A quick comparison with others and you will realize how blessed you are, compared to a lot of people out there. So, count your blessings. Once, when a person was complaining about his old shoes, he saw a man who had no legs. He immediately started thanking God, for at least he had legs to wear shoes, unlike the other unfortunate man.

You may even have fights in your family. Who doesn't? But remember, at least you *have* a family to fight with. There are orphans out there who crave for nothing but the affection of a family. You may sometimes have bitter moments with your spouse, but at least you are married. There are many who want to get married, but remain single throughout their lives. You may not agree with your parents' ideology, but you at least have parents and you are not an orphan.

A lot of people realize the importance of family when they're gone. Don't wait for that to happen to you. Be grateful each day.

Thank you

Get up every morning and say 'thank you' to God. Walk around and take in the unmistakable beauty of nature and thank the Creator who is as beautiful as his creation. When you sit down for a meal, pray and say thank you to the person who cooked you that meal and also to the farmer who toiled in the sun for this to be possible. By doing so, you will find that your food is tastier.

To make this a habit, try a small exercise daily. As you wake up in the morning, just sit up on your bed and start counting ten things from the previous day that had a positive impact on your life. For instance, say you got your salary, or you had a schoolfriend drop by for a visit, or you read a good book. Just count up to ten things and you will feel good at the very beginning of the day itself.

When you start doing this every morning, you will automatically start looking out for positive things during the day and making a mental list of them. This will fill your heart with wonder and grace and this is when you will effortlessly exude a positive energy.

Write a book

As I write the last pages of this book, my final tip for you to have a fulfilling life is this—write a book.

'Me?' 'What will I write?' 'I don't know how to write.' 'Will anyone read my book?'

Don't worry about all that. In life, every person has their unique experiences. If you do not pen them down, they will be lost forever. If Chanakya had not written the *Arthashastra* and *Chanakya Niti*, his knowledge would not have reached us.

Similarly, when you write your book, it is an expression of fulfillment. It is your way of acknowledging a life well lived and coming to terms with the good as well as the bad. It is you passing on your invaluable message to others. It is you saying 'thank you'.

If you ever found out that your grandfather had written a book, wouldn't you want to get a hold of a copy right away and read it cover to cover?

In the same way, if you write one, one day your grandchildren will read your book. You will leave a source with which they will enrich their life forever. And they too will finally say those words to you, words that you are probably saying in your mind right now—thank you.